CW01282824

PORTENTS AND PORTALS
NEW & SELECTED POEMS

ISBN 978-1-913749-65-1

© 2024 Eleanor Rees
Cover art © Rebecca Freeman

Published by
GUILLEMOT PRESS
Cornwall
Printed and Bound by Palace Printers, Lostwithiel

PORTENTS AND PORTALS
NEW & SELECTED POEMS

Eleanor Rees

GUILLEMOT

by the same author

FEEDING FIRE
ANDRASTE'S HAIR
ELIZA AND THE BEAR
ARNE'S PROGRESS
A BURIAL OF SIGHT
BLUE BLACK
BLOOD CHILD
RIVERINE
THE WELL AT WINTER SOLSTICE
TAM LIN OF THE WINTER PARK

CONTENTS

from FEEDING FIRE

The Masque 13
The Back Yard on a Spring Evening 14
Amy's Willow 16
Shadows Talking 18
Honeytrap 20
Telling Voices 21
Feeding Fire 24

from ANDRASTE'S HAIR

Night Vision 41
Roadworks 43
Night River 45
Seams of Dust 47
Parkland 49
Andraste's Hair 51
Sky God Thunder 58
August 60
Winter Dawn 61
Rain-Naked 63
A Nocturnal Opera 65

from ELIZA AND THE BEAR

Merman 87
Changeling 90

Spillage	92
On an August Midnight	94
Walking the Avenues	97
The Knocking	99
A Flower Dipped in Ink	102
Flight	112
Eliza and the Bear	113

from A Burial of Sight

Salt Water	139
A Burial of Sight	142
The Bird Men of the Far Hill	153

from Blood Child

Blood Child	159
Full	165
Tide	167
Dusk Town	168
Arne's Progress	170
Topology	176
Seal Skin	177
The Cruel Mother	181
Blue Black	184

from Riverine

Protean Shift	199
Suburban Epic	203

Nocturne for the Last Bus Home 204
Seafog 206
One Note 207
Congleton Tapestry 209
Mossley Hill 211
High Tide 213
At Gob Cave 215
At Pen Môn 218

from THE WELL AT WINTER SOLSTICE
St Seiriol's Well 225
Bridie's Tomb 229
St James's at Dusk 232
Passage Grave 233
Song Cycle 234
The Bone's Lament 240
In Midsummer 241
The Well at Winter Solstice 243
Keeping the Doors Open 252

from TAM LIN OF THE WINTER PARK
Portent in the High Woods 257
Tam Lin of the Winter Park 261
Escape at Red Rocks 262
Peregrine 263
By the Walled Garden 264
Old House 265

Mothballed 267
Brân in Harlech 268
Divination at High Water 269
Turned Earth 270

from FIVE BREATHS

Five Breaths 273
Quarried Stone 275
In the Woods at Caerdeon 276
The Hill 277
The Cat is at the Back Door 278
Commute 279
In Birchen Head 281
Summer Solstice in Callister Gardens 284
Bidston Hall on Sunday Afternoon 286

Acknowledgements 289

from **FEEDING FIRE**
(2001)

The Masque

Evidently we are between knowing,
between sheets white and clean,
and the cotton habit of priests.
Heavy fabric wraps my body
like a baby taken out into the cold air for the first time.

Looking at the sky though his eyes, I wonder at the names
given to things, consider how I might rename the world
to speak its substance, and then 'tree' would resonate
growth and age through my limbs and boughs.

What I am given are the known names,
yet I know there are hidden vowels in the
pocket of my robe, written on a creased crisp
piece of paper, that remembers the hieroglyphs
inscribed on the inner casing of a dead king's
tomb inlaid with gold.

And how those hollow eyes read the lines as
salt water bubbles from the dry stone face
like a volcanic pool, they wet his history
with what he should have known before.

The Back Yard on a Spring Evening

A gentle drift back through old weather,
seasons crash by,
flowers uncurl and crumple,
light is tissue thin silk soft on muscle.

Years stand hand in hand,
breathe like waves
in a shell roll and pitch into space wide open.

Some children laugh like a tap running.
No fear of spilling time,
or it passing.

A high hilled city
where clouds cover estate houses
like the sails of a ship torn on rocks.

We are not free, are not.
Only rooted, planted by someone.
We are not free, are not.
Sky holds hands around the globe.

Perhaps if land was sea and water wasn't rain
but was light and handsome,
not a heavy smack across the head, sometimes

years can remember, can be firm,
demand to ride towards sharp horizon
before it rusts.

Amy's Willow

spreads light over blue dust.
It calls to the sky to reinstate
symmetry, but
the light falls like branches
in a gale across the eyes
of the little girl watching in the corner.

She sighs
colours the sky with crayons,
laughs lightly when it rains
as the sky is turned into
chalk and streaked like ham.

Fresh meat reminds her of the cradle.
She plays with her sister
like an animal cries when caught.
Sunshine surprises, lectures, and teases.
Her smile is that of an unborn, immediate.
Her world is shaped by
the sun in her eyes and the dust,
blue sparkling dust.

Evidence betrays her, doesn't let in God.
God plays out on Tuesdays when the
winds die down and all is lost.

Her mother says the earth is flat
and father says the earth is round.
They are both right
but the words she talks won't let her say it.

Today they stand on the lakeside
twisting their hair into braids and plaits,
blond, brown, white and red hairdos.
They are the summer,
but the summer can not wait as it fades
from the breath like the final r lingers
on her tongue.

Amy uses spears to hunt across the city.
She is a tiger after gazelle. Among the streets
and playgrounds she looks for what remains
but can't find in bins, in lanes, in time

she may find it but until then she seeks
then hides.

Shadows Talking

Arrival from the dock into Vauxhall,
was truly coming home in a new land;
soil as dark and fathomless
as the earth left behind
in the empty stomachs of our dead.

We existed in shadows and
still are insubstantial as the bellies full of air
our children munched through.
'...I lost her running ahead of me,
she had red hair,
blown out across the mouth of Liverpool shore!...'

The sky is a photo developed in rain water.
Tea coloured light on our tired faces, sears this city's
memory into the eyes of its people.
The mist wraps us into bundles of newcomers,
parcels tied to string our presence,
                    delivered,
to the here and now.

I am still part of you who stayed.
'...I lost her running ahead of me
carrying the sea in a glove...'
The sea, the sea, O the sea

always going back, lifting and lowering
into memory.

I am still part of the buildings you dream, eat, laugh,
make love in, in the songs you sing to celebrate that.
l look for trees, rain, silent places; city streets, parties,
          alcohol, voices,
for some word not yet coined, but will when you recognise
how you still travel when sitting still.

Cobbled streets deflate us. Our eyes are re-patterned.
Curves made sharp, light made dark and the gas lamps
turn Liverpool to cinders and shrapnel.
Fighting for our faces, she was lost before she fell
into the smog, mist, sound of the fog horn on

that river that brought me here. Merseyside, I salute you!

Survival? I wanted more but she was lost at Liverpool shore.
Nothing could be done about it. Nothing could be re-said,
re-worked, re-hearsed, re-claimed to mean remember.
Only the thunder of the children in the playground,
that graveyard where I buried her when we first arrived,
their footfalls drumming out the story I survived.

Honeytrap

    Hands clutch, grasp other fingers
wrap around the bone on
tendon on bone,

    that holds movement in place,
holds it firm,
        un-shifting
like bees caught in a honeycomb
one on top of the other,
        grasp to fly
        grasp to sting
hands hold air tight between
folded skin like fresh honey.

    Knees bend, mountain of knee
pushes sky into shape
    clouds caress
        warm ridges
of skin pushed against the
horizon. Sweat in the knee bend
traps light, makes dark,
makes underground, salt
dries in skinfolds,
    this is the underworld
heart and soul in a bended knee.

Telling Voices

1.

Seagulls inhabit the towers and broken shells of terraces,
the fallen red brick avenues, and the tall elegant
vantages of the rich.

'Watchers — I inhabit you!
I follow you in and out of rooms and gardens,
beyond you and above.

Lovers! I see you swelter in humidity
marionette your limbs into piers, castles, buttresses.

Children sense me and I am friends with cats.'

2.

'...Limit this to talk of talismans.
The colour of the sun as it rose on our first morning together.
The mouths opening and closing as we walked
down the street, dogs chattering
in unknown barks,
the scalding devil of kindness

that brought me to my knees
in front of your kitchen watching your
gown bustle and jostle for space

in the room — because your glow
filled up all of it and held it steady.

I wanted to peel it from you and take
it with me but the wall was
too high, wet and stony so we
met by the railings, in the park by the river and kissed only once
like two birds in a flurry...'

3.

We are the instincts that hold onto memory,
make shapes in the surf in the Mersey
around rocks that little sparrows perch on
half in, half out of wash and scum in
smelly green water that stinks of home.

4.

The haberdashery of taste eloquent about me!
— Who I am what I like, keep whispering
'Julia, Julia' and I tell them I do sweetheart,
 'I tell them' I only wanted to taste you
but that isn't enough.
They will sew me into a dress of sequins
and hang me from the garden wall.

As I cry the more it feels like
you touch me again as

your warm skin against mine
always felt like a sharp stab
into a kind of darkness.

5.

Sunday was a funeral and a sunset.
They pulled me away from you
as if I was falling into quicksand
out on that river — that bloody river,
I'll drink it if my gut could take it —
I'd drink all its capricious lies and suicides —
I'd keep it in my belly free from
tides, sail it internally
through dark and sallow waters.

Feeding Fire

We keep the sea in the bathroom
rubbing against formica like
skin against fur.
Blue carpet, sparse,
foraged by animals at night,
feet trod it
like grass on a shoreline.

Living room a forest, bedroom
a meadow. Kitchen
a sky of clouds
like foam from washing up.
In cellar, a tree stretching long heavy roots.
In attic we keep sparrows that fly
in and out through a hole in roof.

Was it my word against yours about the man in the cellar?
Was it the dark that stopped you looking?
Was it his nicotine teeth barred in the black
that made you set fire to the kitchen table,
dig the ravine in the street?
Was it that when I watched you at night
shovelling tarmac with an electric digger,
was it then, that you decided to fill the road
with water, build me a river to surround the house,
board me up inside to grow my hair, sit in the living room
watching the door to the cellar open slightly,
wondering if the man can see me and knows that you have gone?

At the centre of the house is a tree.
Knots its roots around the foundations,
pokes twigs between cracks in the walls.
Climb down into the cellar, you'll have to clamber
over wood, insects, badgers to reach the gas metre.

At the centre of the cellar in a hole in the tree
is a small man who sits all day stoking the fire with coal
that makes the tree grow.

The small man in the centre of the tree in our house has a
small blue heart which looks like a sapphire but sounds like
a piano out of control.

At the centre of his sapphire heart is a tiny bird,
a yellow canary sings for light caught in the dark of the blue
man's manic beating heart.
At the centre of the yellow canary is a little gold cage.
Its door stops the blood to his heart,
makes him wince, cough, groan.
Canary passes out.

Small cellar man
is slightly jaded, he is the colour of the carpet.

(a distant view of
green rough heather land
streaks his head
     pastoral)

but mostly he is closer to a navy
like school blazers wrapped
over and over again around his
shoulders,
    a small man in a navy
blazer with a mind flickering
(thoughts of) wild pastures,
in the cellar stoking the fire
that feeds the tree, that holds
up the house that
     supports me within it,
arranges the rooms, decides that
they are in the same place
every morning, that that sea
is always in the bathroom,
trees are always in the cellars,
that the river he made for me
out of the road

                              is always
crossable by ferry boat
like at home.
He gave me a city
and I burnt it in the cellar
in the oven, me and the
little man burnt it
                    together
to keep the house warm.

Our living room carpet is the floor of an oak woodland.
Dark room, blocks of light, patterned leaves, ivy bushes crawl the woodchip magnolia. Squirrel claws at bark, bird squawks and tries to fly, hits ceiling. Line of a lampshade grained by beetles burrowing into beige, crawling mites. Moth trapped inside lampshade burns itself slowly, wing by wing slowly sets itself on fire, its thin film wings catch light then smoulder in humid air.

Slapped down on earth soaked carpet.
Face marinated in mud behind the sofa.
Voices talking, landing, hear the ring of voices call softly
'we are trees, we are trees.'
Pull itself up to the trunk of nearest
'we are trees, we are trees'
beating into eardrums
like listening to a ribcage rise and fall,
whilst somebody is talking.

Sofa has vines around it, cuddling tightly,
'Don't get lost in the woods today.'
Ankle pulled into shape by brambles
making their way into the cellar.
A gap of light through the blue linen curtains glances softly over a baby bird fallen from a nest above.

Fingers over eyes and push them into socket.
this is to stop
thudding in head but always people are talking
always every sound ever heard, resounding
like a concave tunnel   banging
trapping   frightened walls
Living box of noise, a box of singing breaking.

In the kitchen the bird hits the floor thud.
Has been flying, smacked itself against the top of cooker.
It squealed as it fell,
                screamed,
'I am falling, catch me I am falling.'

Bird fell for miles the metre from ceiling to floor.
'I am falling, catch me I am falling,'
panicked, wings flapping.

Kitchen built from clouds and dirty dishes.
Fungus on oranges line up in a corner,
old packets of cereal on top of fridge.
Silver and ivory cutlery,
congealed tomato soup lined bowls,
layers of clouds piled into the sink like pillows,
sleeping rows of bubbles.

Bird plummets towards more sky.

House Thinking

'I am brick but they treat me like clay, every day I am invaded. They always leave me on my own at night. I know when they go out in the evening. I ask other buildings of the city to help me. City Hall watches them get off the bus, bars try and keep them standing, pavement walks them home, terrace down the road mutters through windows when they pass by shouting at 4 in the morning. I put them to bed. And they talk of being lonely sometimes. How can this be?

It is only they that miss themselves, only they that hurt themselves. All the buildings in this city support them but they treat us like servants, bulldoze us flat without asking permission. They knock me down, rebuild me, take my street outside apart at night, dig it with an electric drill, build rivers and still I stay with them and don't leave.'

The house is a break of mortar between brick,
smooth rub of cement, old rub of sunned,
rained, made strange,
                     house that holds us,
stores us up in a basin
                  vessel catching drips
of us and we are liquid.
                  Time liquid
pours from gaps in the brickwork
like a colander

spurting years, months, days,
            into the air outside.

This is the rain that never stops falling,
covering the street in petals
that are years,
    pink flecks onto black tarmac,
 form lines and patterns.
Rain shapes explain how time falls

  when it's let out.

Designs cling to houses, shops, the school
                  (this house).
Tracks form between spaces,

    pattern of footprints shows up like
        dusted forensics.
Lines in and lines out of every building
of every space
        (this house).
There are footprints on the stairs
glowing pink, like the town has been
splattered with glitter stuck to glue.

In the dark, tracks can be followed,
like silver mucus left by snails.
Lead our city to our road, to our rooms
to the valley in the porch like a moat,

that ravine in the street,
sharp red cliffs, a rope bridge
strung across red sandstone and brambles
swings in the wind, in the rain.

This house is a biology net.
Butterflies pinned to display cases in the living room,
preserved, noted, listed,
controlled.

Dead baby bird placed onto mantelpiece glass eyed stares
like old toys, sits next to mole and squirrel
all watching t.v. In corner glows out stories and stories.
Power through wire power us.

Dead baby bird neck twisted to one side balances
with wailing rabbit.
Rabbit has three legs only. Trapped by lack of movement
yowls,
'I am here, I am here, find me, find me'
but the house is empty.
There is no-one.
Baby rabbit keeps yowling, skinned mole grins and bleeds.

Bedroom, a meadow. Lie in long sweet grass,
warm-backed against sun soaked earth.
Noise from a road a few miles away trips across fields.
Sky above blue, so blue it itches to be drunk, licks you panting.
Butterfly lands on a dandelion.
Daisy, clover, ants,
there are horses drinking.
Their tails brush the ground when they stamp hooves at flies.
Bed in a pool of daisies.
Grasses grow around the bedstead like they circle gateposts.
Bookcase is a stile to be leapt.
Wardrobe holds clothes hung in fresh air.
Tree at the end of the fencing, buries its roots
down into the cellar, forms rafters, the outline of the house.
Baby rabbit chews silently in a corner.

Hear it thinking, 'eat grass, eating I am grass therefore I eat grass.'
Horses thinking, 'eat grass, I am eating grass, I drink water,
therefore I am drinking water.'
Daises thinking, 'water in earth, earth through roots is water, I
am water, therefore I am earth.'

River runs through the meadow that feeds the tree, that waters the grass, that feeds the rabbit, that watches tv, that goes out clubbing, that is out late at night, that listens for the phone. Phone links to tree, to rows of trees that link houses to house, that pull tightly on the space in a room reducing it in size to the shape of the box in the corner that the dead bird watches and the rabbit's glass eyes glaze like a pot.

There is a fear in the house made of meadows. Hallway is a road into the city, white electric light, lined with bars that heat the street. There's no shelter. Inside or outside. Nowhere left to go. There is man in the cellar and he feeds fire to keep the house warm.

He feeds fire keeps house warm
he shovels coal into glow burn
he makes house held by trees
he makes house like a landscape
he makes house like a home
he makes like a net
he makes house like a cage
for baby bird got twisted neck
he makes moth burnt wings
he makes place feel hot
he makes place feel panic
he makes like I found him in the street

but all the time
he was in the cellar
feeding fire.

from **ANDRASTE'S HAIR**
(2007)

Night Vision

An open moon; burr of grass.
Last reaches of the spilt day
ending, the last
quiet pitch heard
in deep woods. Wet sod of dirt.
Scent of the sun's fire
passing field ruts and furrows,
seedlings, coiled roots, hedgerows;
flight of night-bird
turning tail into a sea breeze,
beak battened to the north.

~

Cloud — now stone in ocean in undertow —
drops from night above the city
into an unseen sea,
at edges of membrane and sinew.
Wade through sky. Perforate.
Pebbles of rain on pitted tarmac
clutter the way home;
night-splashed, corroded.

~

A cold touch in a bleeding house.
An open door. Sores.

And I dream you are the rising sun:

where are your bones, baby? Where are your bones?
    I've hurt for you — for your nights.
    Each turn and flat-packed mile
walked to catch the drift and knack of ends
    and fugitive ends.
Back alleys of the city burn.
Night boils outside the window.
The streets smoulder as morning comes.

Roadworks

1.
Sometime around midday.

The tarmac is biting at my ankles.
Well-lit sky snaps fast and short
as the street opens up to tumble
me into an underground
of corpses and snowdrift
and horses with gold faces
and pretty girls with bees in their hair
and silverfish with steel legs
and smiling boys with tattooed penises
and wet hearts in jars like flowers or flames
and invisible ledges of air
and rock face of baby's faces
and heavy tongues loll like dogs
and tall ships crash on cavern walls
and underground rivers clot:
a golden fleece moulds on a stalactite;
skeleton warriors waltz in the dark corners.

Atop and heavy, Liverpool tightens, glowers.
He disapproves. *I'll be driven out of town.*
A drill snaps down on our skulls.
We shatter like shells.

2.
Sometime after dark.

I know that hurt
colliding as dust
               over bones,

the poor lady's beer-addled bones,

in the dark comes before

    the bee hive city squeeze,

in the street comes before

    avalanche of brick.

Thick blood
comes before

the fall.

My city is wearing costume jewellery tonight —
glittering and unreal.

Night River

East to west, west to east,
wetness crawls

the promenade wall.
Oil and chemical, salt and tar:

the night is in my throat.

I consume distances
at the edge of the river,

three a.m., solitary,
held only by the rain and the sky.

The wind's touch is courageous.

The stars are stags,
antlers pointed at each new shore

sailors discover
far from here, in some sunny waters.

I open to it like a mouth

and sense her shining
full height on the horizon,

as if the horizon is a ledge
she balances upon,

and hovering I rush to her,
her starriness, her electric pulses

that beckon, she widens:

I immerse myself in her thighs.
Her brightness, her size.

I am her: the sea is a boat.
We ride until the dawn.

Seams of Dust

The pavement erupts and the past
— tail twitching —
rises from the cracks.

I lie face down on the road,
cars circling like lions.
A wolf howls on church street.

Two eyes,
yellow radar seeking scent.
Stay still. Keep calm.

Hear the ground break,
hear the ground break open.
Hold tight to the day,
the ends are streaming in the wind.

See the stars in the earth's belly shine.
See the stars in the earth's belly die.

Too much choking my throat.
Be silent now, be silent.

A flurry of ravens sweeps through the underpass,
talons reaching out for meat.
Do not encourage it. Do not speak.

There. It will pass back into the shadows.
Someone has turned the lights on.

It's done.
Take hold of my hand.

Parkland

Skating through trees,
you could break your neck on the moon.

Like a paper doll you expand your body on the breeze,
shadow after shadow.

These versions of you hesitate, sit down,
climb trees, play Frisbee, give birth.

There is nobody else in the park but you,
reclining on benches, naked, smiling,

running between branches, distances,
mending ships' sails on the dilapidated bandstand —

you make rope in the avenues between cherry trees,
weave it round the pedestals of statues.

You wear a crinoline and row armoured carriers across the lake,
swans at your ankles like terriers.

You break your neck on the moon:

exercise horses on the sandy track looped around the edge of the park,
deliver laundry to old women in houses with broken windows.

You lie in the grasses in the small hills beside the streams, touch yourself whilst looking at the sky.

You run naked in darkness across the open parkland, starlight still wet on your back.

Andraste's Hair

    In the woods they are burning her hair —
                      three of them.
    They light it with a match
    and she lets them,
    she lets them burn her hair.

    Watches the ends smoulder.
    Watches the ends curl her curls,
    curl up like leaves.

    She lets them burn her hair.
    There are long dark shadows
                between trees
                   like corridors
    blocked with boulders.

    — The area is cordoned off —

    She let them burn her hair.

    — The area is cordoned off —

    When the sun splits open

    the gaps between trees

and the sun slices into the scene,

they see:

that she let them burn her hair.

    ~

The light opens up the morning.

A plait laid out on the end of the bed
                              like a rope —
several metres long it hung there
swaying,
                tied with a yellow bow.

It belongs to no one now —
lopped off at the nape of the neck.

The door is closed.

    ~

Arms raised to hug the sun.
Woman,
                eyes like sods,
ratchet-nosed, craggy —

hatchet arms creak and clank.

Lady,

sleeping under sunless light,

another sun gone,

reaching obedient: she dreams.

~

From among the ashes,
from what had not burnt,
        gathered to a mass
of brown turf gathered
        her hair
and carried
— a cloud in her arms —
and carried
        to the river
        her hair
to spread in the warp of water.

The light smooth and silting.
The forest behind —
        remember

too much   too much
   dark cannot exist?
    The sun swings to the right.
She went left
   to the river,
    old dirt track,
stepping over grass,
hair taken down to depth.

In the forest they look for her.

Now,

she walks along the path by the river,
her hair in her hands
   to deliver
what had been taken
   to the river,
   to the water —
the smooth strand that curves its path
over the head of the hill.

Something subsides.
Something has passed.
Behind in the forest,
    in half-dark heaving afternoon,
they claw at earth,

scratch around for a trace
                         and further
in the woods
search through evidence,
make lists of explanations,
make lists of reasons
for her absence.

The sun guides steps,
         footfalls —
                 imprint on soil.

                     ~

It wasn't about who was listening.
If anyone was listening
            — to the song not the words —
speaking would mean silence
            — dead ears, dead ears —
but variation,
the pull and placing
in a line brimmed to full
            with evocation —
was almost love and almost listening.

Quiet response to quiet sound.

~

A song heard in the forest days later,

burbled —

made a young boy cry.

Wrapped round trees,
stayed, not moving,
       just hung —
a stopping place.

We could meet
in the woods by the river,
stand eye to eye
in the stopping place
     and wait —
words curdling our bones
     to stone,
  be petrified
       in sound —
a single drum beat, one long groan.

While she walks
a path behind her concertinas,
each stride a fragile weight

that
 pushes up the earth,
turf over grass over turf.

Know how
it is now to be stone now,
to know how to finish.

Listen, she'll break you.

Will you follow?

Sky God Thunder

I have a necklace of blinking eyes around my neck.
The gleaming opulence of foul-mouthed city lights
shift across these fragile surfaces like tongues.

There: high and primary,
like the only thing that ever really did exist,
the moon, out for all to see —

the red of eyes,
thin lines stretched across the pupils like straw.

~

Turf wrapped overhead like a sky
of worms, and a far door in the dark:
the ends of a star
closed tight, it shimmers —
traces of light touching wood,
fat lines in thin navy muslin:
a woman door in a dress of darkness.
The tunnel is long and untouched by lies.
Its blueness is the way back into blue.

~

A striped lane walked towards the cairn,
rain holds my t-shirt to my chest many-handed.
The fields wept; we were wanted.
Lightning cuts through cloud,
a flare from a ship or flashlight in the underground.

In the dry crust of the hill
a cigarette butt dropped by another tourist
glows red, burns black.

August

Just the heat of her muscles'
rich red spasm.

Just the wild distances —
long grasses, horses.

Just the estuary mouth
to kiss at night-fall.

Just the city
ruled by wolves.

Just the dissolution
of brick.

Just the pleasure of rain
inside her

and the wet blue attitude of sky.

like steam from a horse's breath on a cold morning.

Circles conjure.

I can see a man with no clothes
covered in scratches.

He paws under the shadow of an oak
smitten with grasses and insects.

I see two lovers mime conversation.
The sun's death burnt out their lips.

They call softly, love by candlelight,
wallow in silence, abandon language.

I can see him slipping away
into a dark grove of sycamore.

Giant like beanstalks.
Giant like skyscrapers.

I follow, ridiculous,
a clown with over-sized feet,

and enter the dark, sun-hurt, light-whipped.
Darkness smells of sweat.

It is a muscle. It carries time. It carries hurts.
But never breaks or suffers

— a light sparks — a last fallen star in the dark

revealing stark bark edges,
white and black like flaking skin,

then softens. Fire,
the last push of electricity,

spatters torches of heat along back streets
like snakes tongues.

The leaves sooth suddenness,
draw the shutter, pull in the ropes —

and the distant motorway is eaten alive
and the pylon in its compound chaters on

and stones of the wall
that run along

a track to the old farm
glow as if they are

wired by bulbs —

Its lungs are corridors.

I lean backwards in the storm wind
as the river far
hums me a line
from a song he half-remembers

and the high-rise by the park
bends over to the left,

opening up to the stars;
and the garden of the churchyard

mumbles in its gravely sleep,
turns over in a blink,

roots freewheeling into the night sky
then back to earth, unseen, unheard.

And when the door opens
      downstairs in the gale,
            at the entrance is a small child
                  with an outstretched hand.

He will not cross the threshold.
He is from the outside and made of rain.

2.

And still this territory remains imbibed
in sediment that is bone
and leg to sinew, to the lips
I use to touch your lips —

and sinking deeper into years,
with a house upon my beating chest,
the outside has moved within.
I have a day on my tongue
and the night in my toes.

        How this city grows hot upon my surfaces.

I fly in sleep,
    spiralling above the outskirts;
        in a morning walk
            make my own earthworks
                out of footsteps,
  my own edges out of night —
        ritual acts to border the dawn.

In awe
    I place brick on brick,
        move my body
            before the sun
        to know the rhythm
            of the wilderness —
                and make it my own.

Winter Dawn

The city is an envelope this morning
I slide into

and air — a fist of light.

The city is silent and gulls line the parapets
of traffic light lit gables.

The city falls about laughing.
Its sides split

aeons of dust in my mouth.

Reaching into the dawn,
my hands in his belly —

blood red sky, pale eyes.

~

My lashes are twig-sharp.
Early-blue dawn.

The street beats
 unbecalmed, smashed red.

It is felt time.
An instinct.

I can hear three voices
on the air — sunned voices,

crackling and orange —
burnt-edged noise.

Personify a lantern,
impersonate a lantern,

or a streetlamp
on an empty road
in February,

foggy and edged with
circles of rain.

Rain-naked

1.

Underwater, deep and bare,
in rain, in reflection,
sheared from a gaze
lie in wait for me —
in depth,
still, boneless,
in white water.

The fetch and carry of a winter's day
dreams itself weary of us and our demands —
of our weakening and waking
and falling

— these breakings
are molten spieling rain,

of bodies hooked
in the lake behind the avenue
of birch.

2.

The night is shut tight.
The day blinks.
The lino floor of my kitchen
is cold on our bare feet.
We are naked bu these pelts.

The stone drinks in heat
as warmth tires,
falls home, earths,
thickens in sinew.

Our skins peel back to water
and we are blood creatures

pooling in the clouds,
reddening the day's bright cover,
puddling the moon.

A Nocturnal Opera

1.
Setting.

Morning scold of dark
touches eyes shut dark

to see old dark waning.
All shades of dark,

frayed edge dark,
are now hollow head dark

in blue dark now a green dark a yellow dark
outside spectrum unseen dark to give it,

dark, properties of hot wet loose dark —
dwelling in corners

dark under the window
dark in my bed

dark in rooms without dark
window flat glass dark

in the street dark
in flowerbed dark

in gutter, wheels,
parked car dark

in passenger seat dark
church hall dust dark
post box clam dark
closed pub stain dark
rough fist dark
in flat upstairs dark

clambers across beds
downy dark

is brain and moist dark
is turned off dark
is shut down dark
is frontal lobe murmur dark
is neuron whispering dark
is lisping synapses dark
is slow blood dark
is darting dark
is semen dark

of small fry dark
is a jitter of dark
in dark
in dark

in dark
in slow blood.

I set off in the blue-black midnight,
flowers and shops closed and crowded with dark —

in soft warm blue,
barefoot, bra-less,

flung westward.
Day-sounds patter and fall,
recurrence, sameness, abstraction fall to earth

and are remade in the body of the dark,
floodlit, thick-heated night drags on;

thick with sleepers coiled in gluey dreams,
thick with smuggled children looking for homes,

thick with walkers crashing into poles,
thick with ends,

thick with slipwires,
thick with the day's remains.

This skin is a survivor
of too many nights swollen and slippery,

under the flow of a flurry of fingertips.
Touch is an answer to unasked questions.

Touch is a signal, settle, redress, undress.
Touch has many surfaces.

A mouth is a touch moving without destination
through night street's touch of air on a cheek.

The touch is parallel,
result of touch no touch without touch —

past textures gleam through sticky air,
touch faces with your open mouth,

touch fleeting presence with your presence —
touch the ends of days with the fresh touch of your mouth.

2.
Turning.

You lean on the alley wall,

hand on the wall, hand in my skirt.
The alley is dark, the stars lonely.

I come here at twilight
to give life to your mouth.

Brick grazes my shoulder.
The spark of the streetlamp on my pupil.

I am where the curve of your spine meets the night.
I am where the line of your arm crosses the dusk.

I am where the moon rises,
behind you a cool globe,

your face then part of the landscape,
your profile, moon geology —

your eyes are a tunnel between worlds.
'Meet me in the woods' you say and vanish

and I panic, scratching at the brickwork,
grain and grime in my nails,

opening gates and turning over plants pots,
looking into dustbins, disturbing cats.

A bedroom window lamp lights up
'Who's there?' cry voices out into the night.

I slip behind a tree and wait.

Dusk swells. Clouds congeal.
A black cat licks at my boots.

There is a shuffling on the horizon —
aircraft or gun fire.

The terraces are drunk
or dancing,

it's hard to tell.

The gardens are sprouting
thick-trunked oaks

rising.

The earth at the centre
cracks like eggshells.

The forest appears.
It has been dozing underneath the town —

opens up and stretches,
forms cavernous arches

over the houses, over the alleyways, over the moon —
until all light from the cosmos

wells under leaf,
wefts and weaves of leathery green,

a new roof, a new sky — no stars.

I reach along the garden wall,
find my way back down the street

by touch, finger on railing,
finger on lamp post.

They flicker on and off like blinking eyes.
Small pools of orange light

reflect the turrets of trees
that surround the school,

the nursery, the doctor's surgery,
my grandma's house, the bank.

And as I become accustomed to the gloom,
moonlight re-ignites —

a new breath after the shock,
and I can see monks in purple robes

processing past Woolworths,
and a grey wolf howls on the corner.

I can see a baby
swinging from a traffic light.

I can see a child
carrying an eye.

I can see a thin old man
with long hair

running —

his cheeks red,
his heart visible in his chest,
a hot coal in a hearth.

I can see stars piled high as old tyres.

I can see Jupiter's rings hooked on the church tower.

I can see the sun buried in the public gardens,
its red fuzz steaming from feshly dug soil

are a procession of candles.

I run towards the old dark
where the sentry tree

is naked; or more so
is an erection, a guardsman.

The stones glow as if they are coal.
They also are showing me their heart.

3.
Becoming.

In the forest, trees have no substance —
are octopus, flailing blue veined.

The wind raises an angry hand.
I follow.

Each branch is a nerve,
        heating and breaking,

carving and rending
        from fixed state to frenzy

and each hurt is a root
kneading mulch with knuckles

to form a woman — sap-bloody,
new born lost in the forest,

in a fairy tale —
in an old story.

I lift a weary head
from cotton-soft thorns,

eyes shiny and trembling
within blood and wood-born skin:

overheard on the breeze, trees sing —

'to kiss her taste wax leaf sweetness,

hold her to root her so sure,

plant her into darkness,

twist to one stem —
breasts, torso,

a pelvis to turn her —

she buds
and her hair is a halo.

Soil is a cover.
Night is a nest.

Her thigh's width weighs of wood.

Her eyes see centuries.
Her heart knows

rain and sun:

on the inside of her retina
the true angle of the moon.'

O this is green.

Green you move, green
      you so green —
      me under
green
      night so green
   is the green of grass,
green under spotlight,
         green is mute.
Green wells of green,

    poured rain green
on river green,
      a dream of green seeps constant green
beneath grey green always green glanced twig green

new spring green —
O cut grass green.
O green field discipline.

I wake in the dark.
The forest is a hood.

Birds cackle: jackdaw gun gabble.
The cold space between my eyes is green and light.

The moon settles unseen into my skull,
it is warm in these thoughts.

I breathe beams —
pinpoint substance in darkness,

to reassure, to keep constant.
A passing shadow, owl laughter.

I have torn my breath
over leaves,

fallen over mulch dark,
scrambled over borders.

A cloud of air on my lips
taken by the cold.

I wait to return to bone
and journey into the sun's ebbing glue-red.

Breath is an eye —
it sees in time.

Hours trapped in the belly of the dark
tick unheard.

The moon bleeds on a star,
phallus hooked and shiny wet.

Night is a false end.
The sun is a lie.

Red light hungers over the dusk.
An appetite.

4.
Being.

Slow moving shadows lithe in the dark.

The tree absorbs the rain,
drinks the cold,

warms my thinking,
surrenders nothing —

is a patchwork of fibres
like panelling, like tiling,

lets no light in,
eats the light,

strangles the light —
is consistent,

is plentiful,
is absorbing.

The tree, like bone,
has a marrow —

marrow is all my thinking,

as thinking is tired and broken,
has no cohesion,

is swelling up,
is bloated,

is ugly —
is over important.

Thinking thinks too much of itself,
thinking is a red rich blood stain
clotted in my veins —

the tree can thin it with lightning and storm fire.

New ideas of colour,
storm thoughts —

ideas of bark,
an idea of green.

The ideas well and sooth,
are balmy, are oil.
They seep and settle.

Branches at an angle, a crescent moon.

Outside, above, ice forms on the bark skin walls.
I am inside my skin.

Your blood inside me like a system of stars and galaxies.

Your blood in my veins like axe marks on a tree stump.

The outside wells in my roots —
I drift, I sleep; wander through myself.

The nights are subtle, huge and bare.

They confide in me
all their hurried wind-felled dreaming,

the nightmare of dawn, of sun and season.

5.
Ending

I bite my way clean
beyond fibres, beyond bark;

gnaw rat-toothed
at the guts

sap on my tongue,
the blood of a tree in my mouth.

I eat my own bones,
gnaw at my own hand —

jagged and hard-edged.
I taste of aniseed.

I cut at my tongue till it bleeds.

A scramble of insect legs over rock
at night tumbles towards dawn.

I eat my own heart.

When I have consumed myself
the mud is strewn with kindling.

I feel in the wind un-bodied
tissue thin and slide
into the gaps between tree trunk and stone.

It hurts to be free.

Walking the Avenues

I have no lantern to carry
— a fiery globe in the white fog —

across the estuary mouth
to lure sailors to the rocks.

I know that ships are still leaving
down at the river years before

— to Jamaica, America, —

young sailors aboard with their eyes to the shore
and the girls they leave behind,

wild and red-eyed,
skin stung with the bite of the salt and the sun —

while at the end of my road
in today's shadowy dusk

a broad-shouldered man is walking
into the thick fog, into the ether,

and heavy with tiredness,
I carry my steps,

thinning the blood of the air,
taking it in and turning it out

and tattooed by the light
I see pictures in my skin —

the eyes of a rat,
the dog by the gate,

shining from beneath my cells:
this patterned self

is the day incarnate,
breath of hours billows in these lungs

as I fledge wings
and lift like an inland gull

to find only I am tethered
by the city streets —

held so tight
in the depth of rain.

I did not know you would wash away in a rain.

I did not know there would be no relief from the tides
    that pull on my belly day and night.

I did not know footsteps at the full moon
    tapping across the moonlit garden,
        baby hare between your teeth.

I did not know where you came from.
I did not know where you came from.

One night you came blistering smart and ready.

      Rain, some stars, a flat moon

he ran his fingers through my hair

        wondered about

howls and teeth
    that let in rain,

      a thin bitten roof.

You gnawed your way in.

2.

I splash about in the bath.
I lay eggs.
I spawn in water.

I give birth to cubs every month.
At high tide I hatch my eggs —
    and spawn bear cubs in the bath,
        in thick gluey eggs.

They float and then bob up to the surface,
    bear faces smiling out
        from under mops of black wet ears
            to disappear down the plug hole,
    their wet noses and eyes howling,
        'moon monster moon pheasant tide',
            and weary rain drops call us back
    into the air,
into oxygen and felt time —
the cool blackness of a night on the planet
    at the edge of the sky
        just one night: please let us breath.

The bear cubs splash on the tide,
    their hearts brazen and also wild.

You are elsewhere eating liver, eating silver,

from **ELIZA AND THE BEAR**
(2009)

Merman

Eyes wide and water-pleasured,

a silver tail quick in the slip of the grey;
whale-familiar, it guides a man

to land and a dream of home,
to dry nest, stone wall,

static, caught time;
a jar of bees.

He has a tail like a horse's haunches
thick and shining —

and there is no lack in the beat,
in the weaving curl of salt and spray

but still he swims towards the shore
to dry earth, future, past tense:

he swims towards history —
a loose dog with broken teeth.

He swims, he swims,
pummelling new tides.

Stay in the sea, stay in the sea.
Sink your shoulders and fins like a trawler.

(On the sea bed
sailors skulls
skinned by water
stare vacant into weeds.)

He carries bones
in flat motion,

thick felt action
in stroke and oar—

that shore so far
so luring,

he is lured to the shore.

(A fire in a hearth.
A plate on the table.

Fresh fish. Fresh fish.)

A lantern swung by wreckers
at the abandoned lighthouse

seduces his human eyes
beneath a new moon.

His silver fins enclose a depth
of tissue, muscle, blood and nerve-talk.

The meat active and happy,
butting against breeze and pulse.

Heat in his heart, tingles, wells
and rushes on. The land no nearer.

The land so far, so far from home.

Changeling

His body brittle in the dusk.

A full moon on the horizon line
and geese in their triangle

frame the hot red clouds.
His body seething,

shallow and sure,
finds its way out of its skin,

button eyes, ebbing breath,
out of humanness.

Thoughts
flit into the night like bats.

Let them go.
Fall to animal.

A bended paw,
a furred back.

Colours cede to grey.

A rupture in the belly.
Birth through skin not uterus.

Come child,
come night.

Woods far and minerals pulse.

Spillage

Rain-glossed wood,
a lizard's back. Scales

shiny touched by rain —
the whole of the day in each drop.

Under, a fox settles in an oval
of dark dust. Soil

heavens enclose his matted fur
in dryness, head

tucked on paws,
streaked with a film of mud.

On the roof of the earth,
inside is sheltered from wetness

and my home beyond woodland:
room, leather, varnished oak.

Inside here I find blood, marrow,
purple-ordered brain, openings of lungs.

How to move through these?
How to find myself there?

To curl under a weight of self
and sleep at the centre and be sure.

On an August Midnight

                    1.

And there floating in the river of my window
    are faces looking in at me.
In the midnight hot summer dark—
        watching, waiting, whole.
They smile and preen
    and enjoy their eyes
            which glow, two storeys up,
                  in on me here alone —
        searching for names in the glass.
Air is stiff and creaking,
    weighed down by the excess
        of heat and drought.

Rain is days away.
Outside is a jewel.

A prism of dark woods over the horizon
    bellows join us, join us,
        and the hollow by the canal
            is just as cacophonous.
The city needs this look — this hot attention.

It is the house that breathes for me.
I am the outside looking in.
The house takes a deep breath.

The Knocking

   Man at the door the terror
      raps small white knuckles
         on hard wood —
        and pulls his lips in
     and laughs, *no not laughs* . . .
 Small white bones catch on painted wood.
 A man's knocking
       — 4 a.m. and an empty street—
  volleys from redbrick valley canyons:
     and someone has died
               or far-over,
          by the church,
             by the high rise,
       laid out on a bed
        her eyes
              flooded with darkness
                 well lit,
     orange rainy street lit —

and she is a well she has fallen into
        forgotten at the valley floor,
           as the moon gabbles,
              gnarly and worn
       with the day's fat knocks,
         like spitting rain on a slanted roof,

     and someone bleeds in an attic room,
  as menstrual blood's
     slow lava scalds
   thickly down
a pink hot thigh.

Her eyes shut tight.
The night wide open
    and buzzing with fur and moths
      and turrets
         of castles pillaged by raiders

     come from the sea...
     come from the sea...

        while the night shivers
          distracts a new rain,
       from morning's slow crawl
across the river from the east.

It arrives like the ships once did
and anchors itself off shore.

There is a man knocking at the door

     come from the sea...
     come from the sea...

who rips and scuffs the soft skin
                        of lovers high and solid
    in a far away bed.

They lie on invisible tides
         that pull the man to the door
              where he rat a tat tats
                    without groan
           or cough, just
                furious,
from his mouth
      pools of shining air.

Each knock cracks a hole
          in the wall of skin.

The outside is alive and coming in.

A Flower Dipped in Ink

          1.
You came to this city
    from the other side,
from the dirt and murk
of river mud
and cloud

and you climbed
    fleet-footed
over the buildings to reach
my thighs and wet heat.

Sweet child. Amongst
the pigeons and the fuller stars.

We lie in the ardent fall
of black night
on Myrtle street — in the alleys
up against the walls
    we came.
Child.

2.

I became this flower dipped in ink
and the air before a thunderstorm

rich and sweet, the orchids'
fleshly wet skin is taut silk

and my eyes are your eyes
deep in the wet

thresh of the garden bed
and warm ache of damp soil —

curved roots bring us back together
when the night stumbles home.

You hold me like a river
like a valley and a cavern

opening on the side of a mountain
on the fertile slopes,

on green-woven terraces
near the huts and homes

where children run eyes to the gods
and the incoming storm.

Hold my city
in your mouth: a thorn.

Deep in the folds of this book
are the stems of endings,
dry plants are sluices
to hide the light in their green curls.

I dream I pass through earth,
lie upon it; space is rough.

I dream I am dissolved into rock.
I dream I loved a man made of wood

who formed himself into a ship
and sailed across the ocean.

I remember tomorrow,
small hands, afternoon rain.

He dreamt of a new world,
answers, knowledge.

I rest my hands on my belly.
Imagine it swelling, tuberous, full.

The night sky glues itself to the pane.
Breathing slow and serious,

I am reckless, restless:
around me the glasshouse swells.

If we were to stop to let the sky in
and the stove die down

or let the English day have its way
plants would wither, rot and die.

I run my thumb the length of a leaf.
Cry softly to match the rhythm of the rain.

3.
I wake from a dream of you,

my lost son, child with a garden
tattooed on his chest,

standing on a suburban lawn,
naked under the light of the white moon,

and I pull you close, kiss the pattern,
a twist of vines and bright yellow sky

across your collarbone and where
your pulse beats is a bloom of petals

fanned out like a star.

You need to be held like a bowl of water
I should not spill.

The child who needs a heart to hold him still.

4.

I went down to the river and slept.
In its arms, its tides, its breath.

And always there is the other side,
the mist and wrap of spring,

the changing light on water's sheen.

Cultivate this wetness.
First sprigs of spring in the brown soil.

My belly swells in my sleep.
I birth fish slippery over the mattress.

The sheets stink of us
but ridged tough with a first frost.

In my sleep I am gardening —
I have my hands deep in soil,

gripped at the root of weeds,
loosening from the trap of stone.

5.

I dream fire —
mustings of smoke and temper

rise, a phantom
loose around leaves of soft silks

drives the air into frenzies.

Fire in the glasshouse
glistens in the pool-dark.

Somebody breathes in the corners by the inlets.

Remember underwater rivers tidal realms
deep in the depths of the streets of a younger town.

I see the plants shiver and furl,
flesh out their lungs,

green folds stretch up to the moon
and tremble at the hold and hope of the night.

The wounds of the glasshouse are wide open,
a fish tank over-flooding with life.

Lights out in the windows of suburban houses
where young families sleep and dream of day.

I see a young boy wake to the street
strewn with leaf, threads of soil.

Plant pots cracked and split lie in drains.
He opens the bedroom curtains,

round-faced at damp glass,
amazed that the plants have gone.

I see a storm begin, thickly wet
and sweat pour down the gardener's face

as he stands in the open door of his home,
woken from a dream of irises and meadow flowers.

The hallway's light illuminates his baldness.
The pink-carpeted stairs behind.

Whispers under his breath a prayer,
bids them well, his charges, lights up and laughs

    eating the remains of a heart
        on a track somewhere on the edge of here.

        3.

I hear the sun rise,
    a fox's breath lingers in the dawn air
        as it passes into the hole in the fence.

I stand at the doorway
    and weep like a small child,
        my face in my hands,
            my skin crawling with spiders

    that have tumbled out of the woodshed
        and up my arms and over my breast
    and over my eyes and over my thighs
        and into my vagina
           and into my womb
and are spinning webs in the darkness,
  in the wet darkness at the centre of me,
      where I can not see
          and can not touch
          and can not know
              but by hearsay
                  and instinct.

I weep into the blue-black, belly swarming with eggs.
Squat and squirt the red mess over stone.
A soft rain leaves only a damp face,
    tear-coated and slithery,
        this nakedness,
            that sways around me to dampen
            the passing,

as I realise the garden is in the treetops
    and this is a tree house
    and that the ivy on the brick work
    are branches of a giant tree,
    that to fall from here would land
    me in a meadow somewhere
    and there would be a bear in the grass
    and it would have your eyes
    and it would ravish me.

        ~

        O the sun the sun

Rain and a summer storm

        How will you find me?

I will not find you

        the spring breeze an opening
        as I drop back into the city.
I tread on time.
I stand on its back and breath.

        *

Far rush of traffic,
    an in-breath, an out-breath,
        stream steady, full.

Bass notes, starlings,

a rustling car on the main road,
clack of heels on hard tarmac,
gulls gather on windowsills.

This time of day is a slip of a girl
    who carries night in her handbag,
    who lets it fall
        black spilling
      down side streets
          darkening the roofs
of the dusk-flooded town.

To the west the sun is setting,
sinking with me into the dark:

until when you emerge from the lake —
        a shimmer of gold at your eye's cusp;
          in the folds of the lid
    a speckle of heaven.

It skins you, this liquid,
           pulls down your edges —
    eyes shining like a buzzard's
      eyes in a moment of flight.

Love, here's a warm evening,
      we are above and over,
    skimming the treetops in flight —
      hovering like dragon flies —
          our wings also gold and turquoise.

The lake is rich with sludge
and smells of bone meal.

You watch me dip my toes in,
unzip my skirt and slip
down into the thick brown water.

My skin is heavy with moisture,
pricked with heat.

I eat at the mud with my tongue.

as orchids flow, are ghosts
walking on slight roots,

and ivies wind like snakes
and palms stretch out and stride
back to the water's edge,
looking for ships, passage home.

6.
Under a lack of summer
       and storms
and the soft tip of my tongue
and the jewel of my mouth —

under this, sift and flurry,
slide within
a spiel of light —

buries itself in the walls
at the doors
of a room without edges

just eyes and sores
and a cut hand,

a cut like an entry
to run through into

a snowstorm on a desert floor,

into an arm crushed with
pressure of the storm-bred air

and the storm-birthed
at the water's edge,

a pool to dive,

now the scent of an afternoon in August.

7.
From the thunderstorm's
rap on the day and its eyes

blazing through

to where the waters coil,
the plants are rooting

deep into the city's earth
reaching within the heart of rock

and gripping on

as rain bursts
and crawls within leaf and petal.

A dark sky feeds the living.
A dry light hums to the dead.

My boy raises his eyes to the rain,
holds out his hand, catches the light,

as seeds in the blink of an eye
become plants as full as the moon.

Flight

In the small of the dark
he speaks of walking fields,
tracks and winter lanes
miles from here, far in time —
whispers a memory of rain
forty years before this morning
dampens in the bone;
the sky a grey weight
outside the window —

and in sleep
a heaven full of geese
explodes from his skin,
shadowing the dawn
with opening wings.

Eliza and the Bear

1.

I did not know my lover was a bear.

I've seen him bare. I've seen him leave his skin.

He roars. Bear wet, grizzly
      shakes his head crawls into bed
            places a bloody paw on my breast.

In the morning a paw mark on my skin.
It masks freckles, masks my nipple.

I did not know my lover was a bear.

I did not know he was on all fours all night
      crawling the streets looking for the wilderness.

I did not know he wanted to go
      back to woods and harsh brackish skies.

I did not know he wished to go.
He never said,
Sweetheart I am a bear I am leaving now.
I am going home.

The night is a blue green ocean I swim in.

He comes and sees me on certain nights,
        other nights he wanders the woods.

O bite the light sweetheart; bite the edges.

Be bear like.

I can see you being bare as you wander
        eyes like reservoirs gleaming at trees, at weather,
            at colours that spin in your dreams.
When you see salmon,
        the smell of fresh blood
            glimmers in your mind's eye.

I wait for you. I wait in our cave.
I wait in bed, coiled in sheets and red linen.

My hand touches the spaces you made
        before you left for the hills.

I did not know you had gone to the sea.

You took off out onto the waves
        like a landlocked sailor
            freeing yourself from grey sands.

I did not know my lover had gone to the sea.

I woke with salt on my lips.
I woke with sand in my hair.
I woke with the sheets soaked black with oil and tar.
I woke with a gull on the dresser.
I woke with your hand waving in the mirror,
slowly topping from side to side.
I woke with your body bobbing outside the window
on a wave of rain and cloud on a winter's morning.

I cried for your drowning.
I cried for your sunken ship.

I did not know my lover had gone to sea
     until the thunder on the river woke me
          and the empty space in my bed sat upright,
   dressed, put on its sailor's hat, kissed my flushed
        cheeks and ran, unrepentant,
              out of the door.

~

I wake in the night sweating.
There is a figure by the door.
It is the same height as you.
It has no eyes.

I did not recognise you the first time we met
and I should have done.

You were hidden. I could not see you.
You kept turning from me.
It was an ordinary day.

We met in the woods
and your coat was shimmering
in an afternoon drizzle
and your bones shone
through damp fur
like forest fires.

I could see your innards.
I could see your organs billow
and wobble inside your translucent frame.
I blinked.

There were fish laying in wake. Dying
fish wriggling on the dirt path
as if they had crawled out
of the river when you crawled out,

weed angling in the shadows
and a cloud of hot water
as if from a kettle

        steamed on the earth
            you had passed through.

I did not know you though. I should have known.

        What should you have known?

Wildlife, storm clouds, flood.

        What should you have known?

Warm sheets, thunder, breath.

        What should you have known?

Trees in groves, bark and winter greys.

        What should you have known?

Hedgerows, clear commons, parklands, vistas.

        What did you know?

I did not know, that you would come and go.
I did not know you would come and go.

Eating berries from a red paw like fresh meat.

Eating fish from the river like sweets.
Eating the sky with a kiss.

~

I reach my hands into the tides
    and pull out a bear gasping for air.

You fret on the sand for a moment.

I reach deep into the forest
        behind the firs
    where bear paws,
        rough like coal,
            press out from the bark.

I put them to my lips and eat.

I reach into the leaves of an oak
    were you hang in a noose,
        to cut you down and set you
    to smile and soar,
        over the treetops, over the rain
            up and away into the clouds.

I did not know you would come and go.

Will you let me roam . . . . I kissed you

And I turned your face to wind and said there it is go now

and you said 'O but where do I go at night into the blue black to turn my coat to fur and rest my clawed all fours on the bark of a parkland oak'... you sting at the edge of the light.

If you say so

I'll wait for you to leave the woods and make for the hills to follow you... you said... 'If you can run as fast I will be gallant in my far-flung stride. I could travel to the moon on the thrust of each step, each leap into the unknown.'... and gather me home, take me back to the lair...

Only if you want to

4.

I will sleep and wait.
The floor is stone, the sky outside the window
is a blue pane in the dirt on the glass.

I open my eyes and see the shape of a bear
    in the half-light beyond the bed,

on its back legs, it leans on the doorframe,
and smiles, stares at me with black eyes,
        nods its head as if looking at a baby
then springs forwards
and places a wet paw on the end of the bed.

It turns to look into my face, questioning
    and slightly uncertain and then nuzzles
        itself under the covers,
  begins to lick my skin
        with its rough tongue,
dipping between my thighs,
tickling my stomach.

I breathe the thick scent
  of pine forest and mountain river,
damp fur, salt, and sweat.

It curls its head onto my belly.
I weave my fingers into its coat
and hold on tight.

I wake dreaming of bears
and lovers and still the space beside me roars.

I wake my fingers

      tracing the lines
           of its tongue,
               of the sheets' slip on my back,
          the weave of the cotton
slight ridges edging the nub of my spine.

The morning is cold
    as I look into the mirror
and see two eyes glimmering inside my own.

I am carrying myself through the day.

My self balanced in the space between my eyes
    focussed only on the air
the empty places at my left, my right.

I look into the mirror and see a woman there,
but know that isn't me.

I am riding inside her
somewhere on a mountainside

           in the centre of her body,
           in the landscape
           in her guts and blood.

She has acres of land within her skin.

That is where I am,
    washing clothes in a lake,
        gathering berries from a bush,
            gutting fish,
                laying fresh leaves in the cave
        by the stream,

asleep on dry grass.

Somewhere

        in the wet
    heaving dark
I am free.

5.

I have gone to city on the railroad.
I have gone to the snow.
I have gone to the edge of the country
with the taste of a morning on my lips.
I am travelling the distances of red deer
and foxes — tracks in the snow.
My footprint is my signature.
I am tracked by hunters with sad faces.
They run about beneath the white trees like
angry dogs.

I gave birth to you last week

    I roam.

I took you and remade you. You were a bear,
    a cub, embryo
             were sperm invisible.
You crawled back inside
    as I held you, your body shrinking
and thinning in my arms,

    I crawl.

till I have you in my womb like a good meal and settle
    myself to wait till dawn for the birth
in the light of the new sun.

    I run.

a pack of hounds hunts the rats
    in the hedgerows.

Red-coated men on tame
horses clatter beneath my window.

    I hide.

Take off its neck with a knife.

    I come.

and the blood flows onto the soil and fizzes like arsenic

> *I roam in the snow. The tracker's kilometres distant. I reach my mouth into the wet clean snow and drink, my heart pounding. The sun strokes the hills far from here, gently and with kindness.*
>
> *I crouch in white snow.*
> *Sun slight and waning.*
> *Snow borrows from the sun*
> *only what it needs.*
> *There is a row of dark thin trees*
> *on the bow of the hill.*
> *I've sore eyes from the silence*
> *and its shrill song.*
>
> *Night. There is a camp on the horizon.*
> *I circle and prowl its edges*
> *Each tent embroidered with images of animals.*
> *They keep out the night.*
> *Each hare and vixen has eyes darned green.*
> *There are many stars; the fires*

> are red-orange.
> The light has electricity sewn into the edges.

6.
I went to the sea to find your body.

> And what did you find there?

Only water

and you found the cub on a rock by the shore
and brought him home.

I washed him and fed him and held him as he cried.

I put him in a cradle of leaves and branches
rocked him with the scent of winds and wild distances.

> The cub cried.

Out on the shore.

> Whimpered and whined.

Out on the shore.

> In the dark of the night.

Out on the shore.

> I picked him up and brought him home,
> wrapped him in a towel, warmed his bones.

I found him.

> On the shore.

The bear ran away to sea, to find our cub
on the shore and bring him home.

> I brought home the baby.

But there was nothing to eat.

> I brought you a cub.
> I brought it in my teeth.

But there was nothing to eat he needed meat and fish
from the mountains.

> In my teeth swinging, morning sun catches
> on my fur bumbling home with a gift.

Nothing to eat, only the sky for shelter, rain-soaked
    we stood as water poured in through the roof,
there were holes in the roof.
No patches and heat.

> *I can give you heat. Coil in my coat, shelter
> in the shadow of my belly and teeth.*

Nothing to eat.

> *Nothing to eat.*

A snapped wing or neck, ripping of flesh.

> *I eat. I eat.*

7.

He coils in the snow, trapped
    and taken to the city where I find him
one night in a tavern for beasts in cages.

He tells me tales of past adventures,
loves and absences.

I clutch at each raw sentence as it passes into the distance
and I loose their sense on the wind.

He tells me of how he rutted and ran in the wilderness
before the bars and cellars of the city.

I can see him taking lovers.
I can see him taking creatures without names.

I can hear their thrusts, their comings.
their wetness, salt and semen.

I can touch the curves
              that uncoil and wander through my senses.
Past ghosts swell in the dark
    full-eyed voluptuous swaying
        faces wet and steamy
   dancing in the shadows
     as they lock horns
         in the flat black dream darkness
            the dreamt time
  where the uncontained and luminous wretches
     of their bodies tear at our bodies.
The bear cries softly in the corner, a tired smile,
   he drops and groans.

I cry. I groan.

                ~

Mineral rich salt
drips from my skin
puddling and slithery.
There you are on the shore,
walking away into the dusk.

A heavy orange heat clutches
    the earth with hot hands,
      tilts its turning slightly,
   like a snow globe —
   I am hot and cold
   made of mud so
   otherly, otherly.

*

In the woods beneath the pine trees' green,
in the shade, amongst the grasses,
the rusty heat of the new dark
presses hard on my shoulders.

I am in the edge of indigo,
in this evening at the edge of time —
in the centre of the city.
It is my country.
Here in the settled centre of air
that busies gently at the leaves'

flat veins, —
wide open palms
submitting to the sun.

I breathe the bright of the turning dusk.
The openness reaches in,
air fills my lungs. I stretch and yawn.
The light is immediate.
The light is above, within.
It streams, a settling
of time in bone.

The shade around my feet
is loose and sandy.
I sink my toes into the grains of the light
and meld place to place.
I am the shadow.
It is my skin.
I give way to shade and dusk —
thought is too hard, too dominant.
What does the silence mean?

I fall away from it and into brine.
My saliva's salt, sweet and warm.

The silence means the sun is asleep
and waiting gently for the dawn.

TIDE

Behind the railway cutting
curtained windows are still drawn tight.
Aerial masts on newly-tiled roofs
point east: a train from Manchester
scowls west further into
the lock of houses, over the bridge
to the scraps of hedges where the foxes
live border-crossing the line
at dusk to the Mystery and the school car park;
and always down towards the sea
that is pulling all movement out with its
back arched, the landscape on ropes,
the city afloat, dragging all to the horizon:
water at our knees, gulls on the bow.

Dusk Town

Shadow from the bridge slips through curtained windows
of an upstairs bedroom of a terraced house,
shifts across the duvet of a sleeping child
dreaming of the sun, as rain begins again
bustling through clouds like shoppers on Church Street.

In the music store a guitarist thumbs a chord
calling the clouds from cooling towers down river.

A young man who drowned in 1815 rises up and walks
towards his home on Mersey Road.
Water drips from his old bones. As he knocks
the door opens to the fire and a hunk of bread.

Bells ring; the transporter bridge swings towards Widnes.
Boys hang from steel girders, drop into high waters;
a jet plane slices the sky from east to west,
rain tacks to winds from distant seas up stream.

Across Castle Hill, a woman rides a horse into her fort,
woven mantle wet with sweat, a broth in the pot,
as atop the new steelwork of Jubilee Bridge
a welder jumps the final gap to be the first to cross,
legs stretched in mid-air above a rising tide.

Bear skin. Bare skin.

When you came clambering out
    of the darkness
        and ran into the warm spring night
    new forms were found.
        The space between our bodies' rub
was inverted space.

What was made and lived
between us in the darkness?

Where is the blank time
the end time the time after the rain
has settled and cleaned to freshen air?

The day is a dirty
murky swell of deep water: an undertow.

        8.
I cover myself in dry leaves,
    in earth colours so I can't be seen.
So I can't be touched. I will take your touch
    away and discolour it. Fade it,
leave it out in the sun to dry.

I will hide from your fingers,
    from your bear hands, bear touch.
I will hide in the cave that you gave me.
Hide in its shadows and curves
    and replace your curves with earth
and stone and cool nights of dry wind.

An air from the centre of the earth
    swirls from the tunnels like a breath,
as if I am hiding in a mouth,
lying in your mouth,
    carried in the mouth of the bear,
        in the graveyard of his teeth,
    the enamel rich
with old blood and fish.
I'll lie leaf bound. Still.

Your hide is my cover.
    I will hide on the inside
        and you will not find me.
You will not think to look for me there.

You'll be looking for my bones and breasts and hair
    and you'll search the edges of the city
and find nothing.

I will travel like a tiny bird inside your mouth,
    travel with you, tunnel down into the depths
        of your gullet,
until you are pregnant with me
    till you blossom and bloom and billow
with the weight of me.

A cub in the belly of a lover.
A home in flesh and blood, in warmth and animal sense.

I did not know my lover was a bear.

from **A BURIAL OF SIGHT**
(2012)

Salt Water

The river's mouth is sewn up
to stop its ebb and tide, its perpetual pull,

bone dry, thick dry, rough dry —

no more watery reach
beyond the horizon, and our days.

I am a mouth wide open
sucking up the city's sounds:

I need words to wash our wounds.

Every chant, every incantation
is a sod of soil, a heavy weight,

ingested into acid
into blood and marrow

until my stomach turns,
mouths up a fresh spring morning:

as the days rough over my tongue.
I lick my lips. I laugh.

I try to catch the words as they run
liquid into the clotting river,

a rainbow of oil on the surface of the water
a spillage, an eruption,

sliding over the surfaces
on the moon-hauled tides,

and out into the constant depths off shore:
the constant future

where suspended underneath the waves
inside the deep green silence

a seagull's wing beat,
or a motor's hum

or the thud of the container's hull
moored up tight against the harbour wall,

wait for their return at the turn of the tide.

And that water is my own.
I also live inside it.

O hear me call
in the flux of sunlight.

I am not the dryness in the shadows.
I am not a cloudless sky.

I made this song from the river,
sculpted it from wave and driftwood.

O I am abundant and you are not.
Howl to the sea. Howl to the salt.

A Burial of Sight
an urban pastoral

   Sometimes there is another city,
      light and wide,
         shifting on continental plates —
           or icebergs,
             islands,
        ships that spread
          the air around
             the building's substance,
        or pulled apart on rails, splayed out
as you travel
to the other boundary
and take a little of my sight.

I see the journey
      through the taxi window,
   how the trees are a rich-green-rustling,
      your wide eyes
         catching the light
and I, strolling, somnolent,
      downhill towards a subtle river
         know the lighthouse downstream shimmers
        in the sun-brown dusk,
         a flock of terns on the river's pull
    far from here, far over —

He takes her home,
holds her warm.

She was the colour of the winter —
his arms remake her heat.

There is another man that runs
out of breath through the morning streets

to love her, but is made of air.
He hits a wall like a ghost.

He loves only the invisible
world. In the day his

hands settle into stone
and thread straight through

glass, he bleeds
but only rain and air,

the morning dew —

then this evening cool.

*

The light begins to crack.
Couples appear from the path
at the edge of the park
entering into the felted green.

The coolness taps at my skin —
midges, a cough,
boys playing football cry and grunt.
Ducks in threes, a male and two females
waddle over tarmac,
orange feet on grey-black.
She dips her head into the green grass verge,
settles in an oval, wobbles,
waits it seems —
though for who or why I can't say...

Consciousness is a sharp bite
upon us: a hailstorm.

I slip away from myself.

In the distance, the weight
of the Calder Stones
marks the earth.

A love bite
roughed from the mountain's mouth.

Teeth of gods
bite up at the air.

He never leaves. Stone
is bound
and only disappears
in eroded glances
eyelash flashes or rain
across a wet cool back.

Stone man, hard and persistent —
I carved you up, gave you eyes.

The grey sky today has a film
of light behind the cloud.

There's warmth behind this skin.

In the stone circle
is density and crushed atoms.

I dig for your roots so deeply held —

and turn you over, flip back the light,
expose the day in its red raw,

skinless —

*

I am digging up the grasses,
    spading up the dirt,
   tipping up the ends,
      worms and mineral gems.
They glitter in the sun —
are eyes, a burial of sight.

What does it look like underneath?
It looks like the night.
Pinpricks of light filter through churned soil.
    Stars? Yes but also fires
      on a plain, a valley of houses
            low in the mist
    beneath a heavy winter browning light.

From above this soil
   is a meal, edible —
     a mouthful, but within it
a toss and turn, covered
    with grit, a breath of salt
     in a bath of soil.

I bathe in the earth —
   arms like moles plough tunnels into chalk.
Below here the light
   gurgles and deepens,

    pigments my skin with each splash and stroke.

I am buried —
  swimming beneath watercourse
         and tree root,
    crawling I suppose
  but with the freedom of worms.
The roots are lightning.
An underground stream speaks in gentle rushes.

My ears grasp the sound
  and remember the land
    above, where lovers
      are buckling in the long grass,
   feet tread on the carpet
  as I am basemented,
fallow and submerged
in a well of substance.

Why does the substance never give way?

It does in a dream-fall —
a plummet from sky height,
the flight paths of geese above a city park.
In dream I am with them,
solid wings slapping against air currents,
almost like thoughts,
electrical pulses in my dream-soaked brain —

sodden with rest, dreary with a chemical
brew of darkness.

In here I fly, big-handed and huge,
big-flooded and balmy,
through the circumference of the park,
through the blue reaches —
my goose flesh heated and steady,
my feathers a sheen of dusk-light,
brown and white and black.
I skim you. I steal your dreams
and the Welsh hills beyond your valleys.
I swallow them into the beat of my wings,
into the volley, the puck and point —
a transition from north to south.
I fold you into a barrow of air,
bucketing within my wings to bask
at moon-height, the landscape
swelling like caught fish in a basket,
in the crook of my wings' ligament.
I hold it all here —
a haul of vision, all made substance
held close to me, warm and nested
in the hook of my goose heart...
Hot goose heart,
my hot goose beak.

I'll burrow for you.

The Bird Men of the Far Hill

Out on the hill wearing dark like light,
carrying torches they cross the ridge
into the valley's flicker and break,
into spasm of flashes,
triggering moon into absence.

They are watching the river's pendulous hook
against the rust of the landmass,
hoping for endings and clods
of soil to fall sharp
into the felt of the sea.
They are out on the hill, predatory.
They carry heavy stones in their pockets;
cold against their legs,
and are looking for strangers,
unknowns, tornadoes,
in the back of next door's shed,
in the glimpse of your eye.

They gabble, scribe hieroglyphs into the mud
by the golf course, to break open your breath,
seal you within their cages. Feathered bodies
swell at the thought of your quietness.
They want to flatten your thighs.
They want to emit all their hurt.

They want you to take them
until you are as barren
as the winter ground
or as pock-marked as the muddy field.

*

The mulch you find yourself in
is sticky, wet,
filtered mountain, tree bark, excrement.

You are made into slope,

turfed over, never found,
speaking only out of the roots of newly seeded grass;
the football pitch
studded with boot-marks.

You speak into the dusk
    but unheard, now detritus,
        the river drags your remains,
            out into the reaches of the estuary.

Spawning salmon swim over your smallness,
fish scales and meaty hulks
        groaning against your
                dispersal

into salt and sea-vacuum,
          dark depth,

          alteration.

Where is the blood?
Where has the blood gone?

*

Out on the hill they are crowing,
beaks up to the sky yet unable to fly,
sodden and self-important.
They sit on your bones like nesting hens,
shit on your kicks, or tender yelps.

You have washed away.
Every vowel confiscated.
Each final cry taken to market
grown into produce, into potatoes and plastic.
Your parts made into objects
to be equally consumed.

Eat the hungry earth.
Strike through to something real.

You remain in water, or in a field of seed,

or in the packaging in a child's hand
sold to the girl-next-door as virtue.

Runcorn shakes itself down, dusts off fine drizzle;
gulls scatter. In the close-built Old Town streets
children carry church banners on the Whit parade,
molten tarmac sticks to their shoes in midday sun.
Over in the New Town a young couple come from the city
watch the light shift through an oval window.

A teenage boy kisses a pink-haired girl by the library,
as out where the waters widen
the drill bit burrows into the sandstone grit
testing for the foundations of an un-built bridge,
seen only in the gull's eyes it flips like a fish.

In the pub an old sailor lifts a fork on a plate of chips,
smiles as shadows sail along the High Street.
A mermaid, lost inland, sculls through dark alleys,
her tail reflects back the full moon
and the curve of the earth. She dives.

Arne's Progress

Crossing Over

As he sails the coracle of willow and skins,
his bird eyes mirror the moon behind cloud.
Spring tide drags west but he paddles east.
Water seeps through the stitching a little like blood.
Arne buckles his weight over the hump of the river,
the small craft alive on the back of the wave
as he waits for the hook to reveal his possessions:
pot of ink, hunk of amethyst, a drawing
of a storm framed in gold and made of light.

He wraps these in hessian, a swaddle of ornament,
pulls up a line as the clouds move south,
rain simpers along the Welsh mountains,
calling 'Go home now. Find a dent
in the earth and burrow in'. He sings
to the wind, rows the harrying waters.
Across the estuary a ship bell starts to ring.

An Irish ferry slows its entry into the detritus
of objects on the river awaiting the storm:
a broken slate, rat's corpse, torn lace, a mirror,
the thought of the future in a golden case
open to spray, velvet inlay sodden with salt.

        deep in her chest cavity, an inland sea
     sweats in folds of her jumper, sweat on her thighs,
     running to the dark, to the blue-black,
        and on the horizon the seals tip into and out
of flow, are standing on the platform
of the ocean and waving finned hands,
                     flags in the wind.

I spear the night, under-sung
        in the battle of the blue-black
    straining towards dawn,
    as globule rain, teal-coloured, fog-soaked,
        is a heavy oily liquid spooling
      like tide into rock-pools
          and the night takes me up again
   over the bay and into the sky,
   over the marsh around the small town
where on a promontory a tall man stands helmet-proud,
     alert to fresh dark, his hair
    limp with wetness, street-lights before him,
    a succession of animals' eyes.
He picks up an oar, wades through the shallows
    as I am thrown up and over the marina,
over white dinghies moored in the harbour.
          Three men process carrying a torch;
it marks them out atop the cliff.
  Moving slow, a convoy across a plain, past the estate house,

        corn field, sugar beet crop, sandstone church,
        they press on along back roads tarmacked quiet,
    rain thickening. I follow over mountainous roofs,
        skylights' warm yellow, aerials, a forest canopy.
Gables channel torrents
        as the three men are striding along the ridge now,
            eastwards along the well-walked route.
                Their reflections shine against
            a fluorescent poster in the chip-shop window,
            late night offie just locked up,
    owner smoking a ciggy as he turns the corner
        away from their procession.
The men stop and look,
            an unexpected wall, a new-build,
       navigate the underground reservoir,
           stored waves churning beneath thin grass
       pattern edges of the playing fields,
          sail the allotments
              to the A-road again, not stopping
           to look, just on through the gate to the small hill
              bright with sun. Red daylight streams
          from among trimmed hedges as other men
            also helmet-proud step out
    all inland now. Water holds north, east and west.
At a window a girl watches the men speaking in the field.
Her mother closes pink curtains
        and she shivers pressed beneath sharp sheets,

from **BLOOD CHILD**
(2015)

Blood Child

Behind the house a single stark tree,
cherries still ripe though it is mid-winter.
Bletched fruit on bare branches ooze like a cut thumb,
each drop in slow motion falling onto hard soil.
Inside in a silent kitchen, on a metal table, apples curdle
in a handmade bowl; mulched bills ferment on varnished pine.
In the garden, past the pond, the tree stretches
like spilt ink, over-tall, bent back,
to eye a yellow crescent crisp in a fold of cloud.
Black night glass reflects back the dead centre of a pupil.

Blood drips from the mouth of the house.
Blood floods the dry seas of the moon.

On the stained-glass window of the empty hall
red flecks fall, become ice as hail chimes angular
to grey pebble-dash and dripping blood begins to take a form:
of a red-ice-child-creature, gleaming like a ruby
standing silent at the wind-opened door.
The storm glowers behind the outline like a tiger.
It roars but she cannot hear him.
You are not there to listen for her.
The hallway is an empty blue. Books rattle in their case.
Outside she stands like death. The door closes in her face.

Blood drips from the mouth of the house.
Blood floods the dry seas of the moon.

Where are you? Are you asleep in bed upstairs
or running breathless down the street?
Maybe you don't live here anymore?
Are you away in a cottage in the woods
or on a moving train, window patch-black smacked with yellow?
Are you underwater, swimming through
the last swathe of the tide? Are you listening for wolves
at the back of your mind? Are you in a hospital
deep under sterile silver and nurses' blue?
Yes, where are you?

Blood drips from the mouth of the house.
Blood floods the dry seas of the moon.

O Mother has gone missing, she has gone to ground
I sing abandoned at the outskirts of the town.
O Mother has gone missing, she has gone to ground
I sing as wolves' prowl around.
O Mother has gone missing, she has gone to ground
I sing a shining knife in hand.
O Mother has gone missing, she has gone to ground
I sing full-voiced with the choir of the land.

Yes, where are you?

In the garden, the tree flinches, scratched by rats,
the storm sifted from the watercourse;
small muscular movements smatter on a shield of dark.
Cherries gone, turned to child,
who crouches on the front step, red-ice-storm-creature
as bloodied as prey, silent as an unknown song,
as the snow comes along, the tree sighs and bows
and stretches again, under-tall, copying the hill, bends down.
In the house, on the living room floor, a wool rug
turns to water, small boats sail to wind-fed shores.

Blood drips from the mouth of the house.
Blood floods from the dry seas of the moon.

Are you underground, in the cellar or soil,
hiding in the mulch and leaves? Are you rooted
in the dirt or rolled up in the rot,
heart beating slow, lost light in your eye?
Or are you in the wood pile, kneeling under last year's pine
needles sticking into folded skin, or are you
gone from here, aloof in the wind like a wild goose
journeying south from darkness, garden soil
untended, land unturned? Are you un-become,
laid bare in the last light of winter sun?

Blood drips from the mouth of the house.
Blood floods the dry seas of the moon.

In the kitchen the tap drips a slow, red drop
onto stainless steel clouded with washing-up sods.
White light filters in through an open window.
Outside the garden heaves in wind; one breath.
A figure runs along the alley, a child or fox
but closer, starry red, her bright face at the glass.
The tree paws the soil like a horse, a branch
turning over loose earth with a sway, a lilt, a whip,
a crack but only as far as its roots will allow.
What is the spell that holds them still?

Blood drips from the mouth of the house.
Blood floods the dry seas of the moon.

It is the spell of silence,
child, she doesn't speak to the house.

It is the spell of silence,
child, she doesn't breathe to the frost.

It is the spell of silence,
child, she doesn't sound in her throat.

It is the spell of silence,
child, so she doesn't feel the loss.

Yes, where are you?

And the rats run to the river and the dogs
run to the river and the chimneys spark like kindling.
From far west flickers a firestorm through the town,
soot and smoke, sea buckling in distance,
a hot avalanche across frost-crested rooftops.
The red-ice-blood-creature waits on the doorstep,
listens for a high pitched wail from the garden;
fat of a song. The tree is whipping hard
against the fence, it cannot run. Branches
stacked one on one form a shield. The fire comes.

Blood drips from the mouth of the house.
Blood floods the dry seas of the moon.

The house raises its head, tips back its neck.
In the hall a vase falls south, a ship in a storm.
Empty glasses smash their silence inside the kitchen cabinets.
A knitted doll tumbles down stripped wood stairs.
And underneath in foundations bricks
plough down into sandy earth like a rudder
and the bow of the building turns for the river.
The roof flips like a flag and the whole house
dredges through the molten earth which parts
like waves, splitting the garden wall, tarmac road.
Inside the schism, tree roots hang like curls.

Blood drips from the mouth of the house.
Blood floods the dry seas of the moon.

In the wall of mud, each frond turn, forms
a human face, oval-shaped, which calls out, *Where are you?*
Fire on the horizon crumples church-towers
as the red-ice-blood-creature starts to drip and ooze,
a snowman after snow has gone, warmth
scythes the sides of her small girl shape and becomes
a spring, a stream, a brook, a tidal river shifting mud
and roots to form a gorge with wooded sides;
through leaves two figures run, girl and woman,
each a ruby mark amongst a basalt green.

Blood drips from the mouth of the house.
Blood floods the dry seas of the moon.

And their melting blood flattens the fire.
At the crest of the ridge, as large as the sun,
lamp-lit town below like embers in the hearth,
steam in the street now quiet as cold the woman
who was a tree reaches out a hand to catch a crescent
painted onto navy cloth, tilts it back and forth,
then picks up her child, the red-ice-blood-creature
and pours her like lava onto the crust of the moon,
staining it sticky and the light spills like wine over the valley,
and a single cherry tree, in a garden, behind an empty house,
the fruit still ripe though it is mid-winter.

Blood drips from the mouth of the house.
Blood floods the dry seas of the moon.

Full

Moon-raked, unable to sleep,
I wake landlocked
and unwilling to shift beyond
my own horizon
into a fall of snow, or a tired
embrace, or a landscape
of ships and sails, old relics
on the shore, or your hand
again or the draw and wreck
of the sea on coastal plains
that is lapping even now:
2.35 a.m. late, unearthed
and deep in a city's sleepy silence
that's remarkable and unsung,
no trains, no rush of cars;
just this flat moment
heavy in the black cloudless sky.

The church on the hill
squats in a square of shadow
under the moon-ridden moments
of shifting white, and somewhere
inside perhaps near the altar
or in the pews she is sitting
alert to our dreams, hat on

for Sunday, hunched forward
in prayer. The door creaks
as I enter, sleep-frenzied
and aware of the turn of her neck:
her startled eyes
in the shadows witness
my night-time intrusion
into the life of the dark.

A handful of red hair floats like a jelly fish
caught in the to and fro, in the froth of the drag.
A cormorant extends its shining black feathers
as he walks ashore on the bone of the wing.

St. James's Infirmary

In the graveyard the children have cholera.
They lie on stretchers, on iron-framed hospital beds.
He is mopping their foreheads with mildew,
parchment, moss, quietness and winter rain

which he did until just before dawn;
long hours of talk, laughter, occasional song.
The light from the moon made everything white.

He gave them gifts of fresh river water
and they drank with their mouths as silent as stars,
small hands cupped around the tankard,
milk teeth tapping on the cold edge of copper.

Philharmonic

Arne listens to lager fizz in long glasses
and talk of staying out all night.

Tomorrow will be sleeping in,
hot breath, sweat, some slow love
amongst well-worn sheets.

But tonight under the chandeliers,
tiled walls, silted green, a haul of banter
caught at 5.30; the river's tide still high,

a violinist plays Dvořák in the shadows
as the bargirl takes his order in Irish.

Cortège

With reins folded under his third finger and thumb,
black horses high-step oiled hooves,
feathered plumes braided to their bridles.

The avenue pulses and flames, and windows smash.
A lad struggles forward, head bloodied.
A police van screeches round the corner out of view.
The horses do not bolt or flinch but hold their heads up high
as a parked car ignites and burns out in a breath.

Arne gathers the embers and tar into a jar.
The ashes he places in the back of the hearse.
Spring flowers entwine SISTER along the coffin lid

and on he drives as lamp-posts scale back
from sodium to oil, and a setting sun dampens the fires.

A bulldozer gouges an end terrace's eyes,
as an old woman in her kitchen watches through the window,
a cup of tea in her shaking hands,

and on he drives over cherry blossoms splattered on tarmac
while a man at the bus stop scrambles through a sandstorm
to a hut in the village where a brother was murdered.

At the traffic lights an 80A pounces from the junction
and ploughs straight through the oncoming hearse,
his horses enjoying the sensation of diesel,

sweat and steam in their bellies, in their long flowing manes.
They emerge on the other side
still composed, still clattering home.

Sheen

A seagull is flapping its wings in the glasshouse
as Arne stares in, globe-faced and shining,
at tables laid for dinner under the height of the palms;

and as the bird rises the vaulted roof blossoms
then derelict again, window frames reveal grey clouds
to wedding guests observing the gull's flight into time.

Yet the marriage is still perfect, transparent and glowing.
A spun-silk bride, a cake opaque as ice,
a slow first dance amongst the exotic plants.

And as he watches the glass house spin on its axis,
marble botanists in the garden slowing the sway
while white doors break open, cough jasmine pink petals.

Arne walks among the scent of salt and manure.
Heat sweats his vision, colour drips to the floor.

Magnolia

Arne lies watching shadows
waft across wallpaper,

hands behind his head, toes to the ceiling
on the slightly-soiled white sheets

until he begins to seep again.
A draft blows through the corridor,

catches, and he is away into the brickwork,
mouthful of mortar and plaster

in his stomach's translucent core,
a bright sack of minerals digesting into dust;

and then he is on the decking, waiting,
while rain drips through his contours

as he lounges on the garden furniture,
rotten wood swollen with fungi.

The parkland beyond the trellis
brims with water;

a woman with a pushchair
runs into a shelter.

He pours into the rain, holds her hand.
Lets her breathe.

Topology

I dream you in your sun-watered garden,
a route to us years now gone,
then walking through the trees to the lake
and my immersion in you and the light
on the water like you

and how we are made by the turns of the earth.
Still you are as steady as clay
and I shrink to you, in each step,
each lengthened moment of our meeting
stretches, until, unnamable

after no time I am without time
back in the stream of us
walking through our city, which watches,
then melts to new substance;
remember the girl's cry as she ran too close to the edge?

And yet the river slides on and I cannot stop its push,
unfathomable, unlit,
                into the flux of us,
                        completed,
                        continuous.

Seal Skin

Sun shifts through the clouds' broken shade.
A red fox flits like a bee.
She runs as fast as the east wind blows
from the motorway to the sea.

In the house at the edge of town,
her family keeps within
a girl's shape in a leaded jar,
the memory of her skin.

    Her body forms from shifting sun,
    cloud water becomes a lake.
    As she runs like wild earth turns,
    leaves from the spring bud ache.

And she runs without her skin;
a glimpse from a passing train,
a shimmering ghost in fading dawn
through the bracken by the lane.

She pounds the frantic carriageway
like a hunted deer
weaves amongst the cut of cars
yet only he can see her.

Her body forms from shifting sun,
cloud water becomes a lake.
As she runs like wild earth turns,
leaves from the spring bud ache.

And he knows where this will end,
turns the key in the car engine lock;
glances again, breathes in and out,
the horizon in his look.

And she runs like the wind is full
in the sails of a tilting boat,
calling to the land as she goes,
New buds make me a coat.

And calling to the land as she runs
Clouds give me your grey faces
like a sky before the thunder
sticks to my open spaces.

And calling to the land as she runs
Soil in the tractor's furrow,
give me your warm damp earth
your grainy dark tomorrows.

A field rises like a swarm of flies,
till drenched in mineral-brown,

throws dry earth over her bare shoulder.
she is strata like a mountain.

> Her body forms from shifting sun,
> cloud water becomes a lake.
> As she runs like wild earth turns,
> leaves from the spring bud ache.

He turns the car into the single track
which leads towards the gate.
A no-entry sign swings in the rain.
A gull perches, quietly waits.

In the oil-seed crop she runs like time
and on through the silent yard.
Fattened pigs all kept in lines,
hens held in sound-proofed barns.

He stands on the muddy track
as she comes, mesh of leaf and soil,
rain heavy as the ocean floor,
her belly bulbous as a seal.

And blubbery and flecked with grey
his skin a soft furry sheen.
He holds her in his arms and sighs,
You run like you can swim.

Across flat fields pours the sky,
sea escaped from a bulging coast,
culverts swell till they burst like stars
and the two seals are submerged.

      Their bodies shift with changing tides
      and strong-born waves begin.
      They swim like wild earth dives
      as salt crystals encrust new skin.

motorway's throb a distant heartbeat
    and I am almost asleep,
        turning through grains of dust
            which trail my flight across the peninsula
    to the crematorium by the roundabout.
It still glows raw and red.
    I see a man leaning on a gate,
        small knife in his hand. It glints
        as I leave him to his darkness.
            He is raging into the blue-black.

In the brook diverted beside the railway, muddy
        but swollen with excess rain, two
    children bob along, heads held high, clamber onto the bank,
        sit and let their legs dangle into depths,
            stare straight ahead, then dive.

At the corner of the out-of-town car park
    she pulls up, runs, pushes through a hedge,
        but the children have sunk back into mud.
I can see their outline from above.
They are giggling, lying like flat fish beneath the stream
        and over towards the woods, on the ridge,
            past unknown bones in breeze-block stables,
                over horses, one leg bent, stone-still,
pegged across the slope, a dark dun pony in a blue
    blanket eyes my flight across cloudless, end-paper sky.

On the line of the hill
    a cry strikes. On the mulch, blood stains
        into leaves; a man's body in shadows
        slashed hard, slumps into bone in seconds.

I rise above the hill, this red hill, green fields
    below dotted with men in battle, fighting hand to hand
        with spear and shield. They are

        battling amongst the telegraph poles
        battling amongst the ploughed earth
        battling amongst the tractors, parked in the farmyard.

Each man blooded; an inland sea.
Each body dissolves to soil when it hits the furrows
    until the field is emptied of flesh
    but runs red, sharp scarlet;
        a yellowed autumn day
and a young man feeds hay into a harvester,
    then gone, just darkness and threat of dawn.
Blue-black weight is the night,
    seals redness into brown earth
        waterlogged with too much rain.
Field a fen; crop rotten,
            and through blood-clogged dirt
        two children run as if into the sea on a summer's day,
            laughing, hair streaming scarlet, mahogany

At Gob Cave

I return from the crouched stoop of the interior
securing my tread on the slippery broken stones

over sheep droppings, brown pearls on green grass,
to the vast valley's openness;

a funnel of cars slides into the sea and the clouds
flapping grey crepe drying in the wind —

a red tractor drives in lines below, startles the sheep.

Behind, within the cave mouth, slant-like lips needing water;
a smaller fold to the back with room for a body
to be laid out, a female head tucked onto a chest, toes
to the ceiling, stillness and dust and quietness —
quietness at the hollow of the hill,
No movement beyond down — no up and out —
       flesh to putrid onto bone
       and down down into dust.

A stopped movement and silence — still, dry space
in the crack of the rock, a deadening of sound.

*

Out here, a chestnut pony stands amongst the gorse,
lowers his head, raises grass from the roots.

The hill under me holds the handprints
of all who brought a rock to the cairn.

Like them my body wants to change dimension,
to become something other than this form.

I cannot change my bones, or fat or marrow
without dying into stillness, darkness
like my skin held in the mould of the water and remade
from dark to light, hot to cold
all absolutes, the God, the dark, the death
a transition: a passage between poles; points of a map.

*

At the centre of the cairn, subsidence
like a bruised head or mine shaft implosion,

wild thyme's small purple flowers,
tiny lichen yellow on grey stone, wheat grass tips.

Remember though woman, below,
always inside, under and at the centre of the hill:
she rots in the stillness of the fold.

The Cruel Mother
after the ballad

Amongst the leaves I lie
teeth-bared,

raw as the sundown.
Scattered skins hang on the trees

like prayer flags — I am demon,
I am the bad-one.

I am the wild, edible bark.
You bit my tongue and made me roar.

I will barren you, bust up your eye,
scratch at damp dirt with these claws.

Where are you? Nest of twigs,
den in the woods,

hut with smoke at the door.
The home burns its riches.

My young slide onto the forest floor like eels.
They writhe —

branches hold them. Swaddle
small forms with dirt. They call

on into the blistering night.
Sky bubbles and caws.

Trees like dogs lick at the sun,
wide as horizon, large as moon.

The oak I lean on leans back,
bark like a spine.

Over the fence on the well-kept lawn
I hear them talk —

O there is nothing to be done,
nothing, nothing to be done.

And hear him say
It is not his fault.

And they all agree
it was all up to me.

In the green wood
I sing to hope of rain.

I sing to blood
which falls and pours;

in the garden they sit, drink wine
and thunder, wonder

where I have travelled towards
but don't stand and search

but talk, and worse they sigh,
O there is nothing, nothing to be done.

I will eat these babies,
cook them one by one.

The green wood says I should stay the night.
The green wood casts a curse

on those who say nothing can be done
and leave me, a wild cat, to run

into their sleep in hot damp beds,
into their eyes in the dark.

I am a clawed mother
and he will not have them back.

O the cruelty he weighed on me.

Blue Black

> ...*coming ashore in the wilds of the Wirral,*
> *whose wayward people both God and good men*
> *have quite given up on...*
> —Gawain and the Green Knight
> trans. Simon Armitage

> *The Norsemen left them in their well-nailed ships,*
> *The sad survivors of the darts, on Dingesmere*
> *Over the deep sea back they went to Dublin.*
> —The Battle of Brunanburh

Yr wylan deg ar lanw, dioer
Unlliw ag eiry neu wenlloer,
Dilwch yw dy degwch di,
Darn fel haul, dyrnfol heli.
Ysgafn ar don eigion wyd,
Esgudfalch edn bysgodfwyd.
Yngo'r aud wrth yr angor
Lawlaw â mi, lili môr.
Llythr unwaith, llathr ei annwyd,
Lleian ym mrig llanw môr wyd.

Truly, fair seagull on the tide,
the colour of snow or the white moon,
your beauty is without blemish,
fragment like the sun, gauntlet of the salt.

> *You are light on the ocean wave,*
> *swift, proud, fish-eating bird.*
> *There you'd go by the anchor*
> *hand in hand with me, sea lily.*
>
> —The Seagull
> Dafydd ap Gwilym, trans. Hopwood

Before this I was a gull.

I flew from the city
    over the blue-black estuary, along the shoreline
        towards the abandoned lighthouse.
I flew through the wind-farm's rotating blades.
I flew over the river's rain-battered sheen,
    sodium spots lined up into a pattern
        of a peninsula's edge, fairground-lit,
    houses strung along the coast like lanterns,
a black-railed prom stretching to distant
        heavy mountains, marshland and flat fields
    backing away from the sea wall, grazing cattle,
a long tarmacked path through trees
    to the beach and submerged forest
        off shore, deep in sand,
    shimmering white transparent woods vatic in the waves

and with my gull's eyes I watch from above,
    from up here, on the air currents;

the children are two black dots
running over the shingle from the dark night's sea
towards a woman on her knees
in the moonlit sand, wide-opened arms
as if she is holding a towel on a summer's day
though it is a December's night. Is she me?
I look through her eyes to focus on the children.
A girl, a boy, naked, about six and three:
faces fuzzy around the edges,
with hair and eyes but no definition,
they just keep running over the wet sand,
sea rough behind, outline of a container ship on the horizon.

I try to fly inland towards the ridge
but air currents push me back towards the edge.

*I am kneeling, arms outstretched, squinting into darkness,
small pale bodies running towards me.*

I am hovering over the shoreline, over the estuary,
children running over wet sand, a woman on her knees,

then she's walking to dry land, shingle in her boots.
I follow her return towards glass-sharp dunes.

And she drives, her hands fixed on the wheel,
two empty seats in the back of the car,

  shadow splashed on ripped upholstery,
    seat-belts swinging, turning to the lights,
      a three-eyed wolf at the edge of the track,
  and the road ahead wet and sandy,
    pitted with last week's storm.
  An easterly catches and I am among flooded fields,
    webbed feet tacked onto moulding wood
      as the vehicle rolls out of view
    to the cross-roads by the motorway.

I'm flung north,
  each wing stretched into darkness
    above a house with one light in the top floor window,
      and there she is parking in the driveway,
    closing metal gates on the semis across the street,
  opening the front door, curtains full on cold glass.

I can see her unpacking a bag on a table, turning
  on a radio, staring out of the gap
    in brocade straight at me
    here in the blue-blackening edges of the sky,
      suited to this rain that starts again
    and up and away
      behind her, behind me into the curve of the land
      about a mile beyond her home, car, fence,
  and further out at sea
    tide turns, a stone wall rises

                    from beneath green swell, marks out
                            a harbour wall, long smothered
                    by salt, where a ship is moored,
            unloaded, a clinker low on fine water, well-nailed
                    steam-bent oak and pegs, a carved
                            dragon's head on its prow;
            voluminous sea subsides to sand
                    then marsh, then earth, brown-furrowed mud
            and chariot-tracks, mastheads clutter distance,
            a barge steadies on the tidal flow.
            Sunlight blasts the scene with coppery emulsion.

She closes floral curtains; waves filter detritus.
Drowned plastic bottles sink into coarse sand.

        We are with her in empty rooms
        and fossilised nights.
        We are with her on blank blue
        afternoons of silence and repeat,

                sings marram grass to the wind,
                        blowing dunes into back gardens,
            flicking shingle scratches onto conservatory windows,
                    catching feathers which turn me around
                            and over the shore. In the shallows
                                two children still play,
                        throwing sand at each other's eyes.

The night is an owl, round-faced and poised. It hunts
        mice in the rape seed crop
    behind rows of pebble-dashed houses,
  sliding doors level to a new-laid patio.
She is eating at the kitchen table,
    spoon into bowl, to mouth to spoon to bowl
      and return; behind the extension
    in an upstairs bedroom, mauve curtains wide,
        a man rocks between the legs of a red-haired woman,
his hands on her wrists, she laughs.
They put out the light.

As the moon slots itself back into the jigsaw sky
    I am over fields again,
      pulled towards sea's rolling dark;
  and at the shoreline's square corner,
      deep under high tide,
        prom abruptly halted on the beyond,
          a small island and mountains,
      waxy waters weave amongst red sandstone
of eroded land licked off into suspension;
      water bubbling, iron-bitter,
each return rubs sand onto sand
    and rocks beneath water's hold
      stratify into auburn folds on fold:
erosion precise, waves expand
    spaces, small fish

        turn within sudden shallows,
            flicker tender silver bellies to the moon;
     and I am upon them, reaching hard
        into cold wet spray, shimmer,
      rip, salted blood and sweetness.

Wind fastens itself to slippery land.
A car on the coast road coils towards the marsh.

A fish shines out at sea.
I survey and flinch, a creature far away,
         a seal strayed from the island's shadow side.
But looking sharp I see two children
       swimming a gentle breast-stroke
          through black water, as if in a pool.
           Serious-faced in parallel they dive and flip,
        small feet flicking into air like tails,
          and emerge several breaths away
    towards the horizon-line and endless dark.

From the gatepost I see her running,
    car stopped suddenly on the verge, door flung open,
       running, long hair static in wind,
       running across the beach. Her feet
         drown in dry heaps, until on wet sand
   she is running towards the sea, her face
      flushed pink, blood rough

     drenched skin. They seem to revel in it.
     A car howls away towards the coast.

And the ships on the river sail for the north.
And the barge on the river sails for the south.
And the sun in the east sails for the west.

She drives below me,
  her eyes fixed on the road.
Wipers tic as she waits at the lights.
   In a front room of a pebble-dashed house,
     one stray lamp on, a woman
       stands by net curtains
   watching more rain and a passing car.
    She holds a model ship,
      she rips apart slowly,
    tearing thin cotton from the rig and the mast.

And I swoop away over our ink-written shore, swooning
  through full wetness
    and double back. I loop, I cry
  at all movement, gaping sea
    hurrying towards me.
  I crash in, diving beneath the rough of the flow.
Within folds, blackness slips
  and swims. Hunger-driven,
    but not rewarded I float

beyond the island as wooden ships
are leaving. Sailors
heave oars into cut sea as I dive again,
returning, fishless, but coiling north
around plinths of turbines
the boats navigate like sandbanks. Being opaque,
the crew need no light, cannot
be seen on radar or from the tanker
churning its way into the wide estuary mouth,
though the long-ships' glimmer,
on the local ferry's glossy hide.
And from the ocean I can see her
take the marked track across massed dunes.
Mascara in her eyes, she wears a thin coat,
keeps moving through the dark terrain
to a turning towards the beach,
watching felt night, listening to my call,
following high tide and a bold moon;
and on the north shore, from the lighthouse
she is running to the blue-black,
then kneeling, arms outstretched
as if on a summer's day
for two children bobbing on the tide.

Gulls in the storm,
gulls on this tide,
beaks wide open to catch her breast,
she lets open to the rain.

from **Riverine**
(2015)

Protean Shifts

    I am digging me. I am swollen spore
          swum in the slow tide south
       towards the shore, dredged from
            the wildflower of the Thameside.
I form on the skin of bent-double men,
      unearthing the hollow of me,
          pick-axing mud in a spring storm
      which does not stick but slides
          into their lungs. They breathe me
    home to their wives, into mud,
              children born of the canal-side.

Barge's red-flowered painted swirls
like the lick of a tongue
around a glass of clean water.
I want to go outside but I
can't go any faster.

I am digging me. I am swollen spore
    like a gull at sea on and under
        to the black water bubble of the navvies'
    continual thrusting cut at the rock
        in the sharp heat of endless summer,
    their sweat like stars on a shoulder's shift
        from pick to impact; I stick
to the pelts of mud they wash later,

    whiskey on their lips.
 On the quick route home, a young man
    splashes canal suds over his bloodshot eyes.

Barges' red-flowered painted swirls
like the lick of a tongue
around a glass of clean water.
I want to go outside but I
can't go any faster.

I am poured. I am moored. I am run.
 I glimpse in the shallow loam, a rat
   sculling its way through the parallel bricks
 lined with moss and mud. Down under
  a coin punched into the sludge
    sparks as the barge's bow
   glides over like a seal's belly in far waters
 O marine radar. O transatlantic passage.
 O epic journey across the Atlantic.
 Where is my north,
       my tidal surge?

Barges' red-flowered painted swirls
like the lick of a tongue
around a glass of clean water.
I want to go outside but I
can't go any faster.

I will never know you, glacial melt,
    felted as I am in earth. I settle lower
        into the legacy of dirt, appliqued onto midlands'
    green, afternoon teas, farmyards' midden,
        and country fetes. A vicar with rosy cheeks
walks towards me offering his hand.
        I smooth my line towards industry, the north,
            riverine estuaries, coal-dust, turbines.

Barges' red-flowered painted swirls
like the lick of a tongue
around a glass of clean water.
I want to go outside but I
can't go any faster.

I am digging me. I am swollen spore
    flooded across the un-drained fields,
        stagnant water in molten pools, a roof far gone.
    I return along roots of the beech wood copse
        through thick mud and rotten crops
    until I swell overblown and ripening
        through the sluice, into the lock
        where a small child swims ragged-faced
and long-gone drowned, his skin
        like a fish's gills breathes for him as he dives.
I know him in me. I feel each final gasp.

Barges' red-flowered painted swirls
like the lick of a tongue
around a glass of clean water.
I want to go outside but I can't go any faster.

Suburban Epic

The red-eyed man has a face which flies north, peels
off his skull like bats' wings or folded paper caught
on the rain-driven wind from the sea. His eyes
gleam through the sockets, he smiles like a song,
leans on the gate outside the tight-lipped house;
bare arms on tarnished metal seep up the dew.
He waits. I walk towards him from the front door,
but falling back into buddleia at the edge of the road,
inside its willow basket I am encased in hands
which rub me like a child in a newly run bath or a grave,
and I plummet until upright and the red-eyed man stands
again at the gate, now with a face. He takes my hand
and we run like missiles through the dawn-raided side streets,
curtains buttoned down, all eyelids light on retina,
to the track into the woods, the bridle-path to nowhere,
and he purrs beneath his breath as we mate,
him behind, me on my knees. Blood spots the parkland.
Up against a tree bark swallows us, crisps over our pulse,
forms our breath, him in me. We are coppiced.
Day comes, he vanishes; we are two branches.

Nocturne for the Last Bus Home

City, before dark comes I want to sing for you, name
all net-curtained windows one by one.

All your lights turned on for an evening meal.
I want to speak your bevelled iron gates, the ring road

in full voice: a spring evening and I am full of you.
You give me whole numbers: 'up since four,' says

the woman getting on, as the bitter air breaks us
on the top deck, to the hilltop, through Fiveways on the ride

to the hospital car-park, past contracted breaths, sharp pulses,
a couple happening in the folds of your alleyways,

or the rip of skin in the maternity ward,
or on to Knotty Ash: a dragon on the playing field.

O crumbling darkness, come now come, to the blue glow
of TVs in a back room pushing across the perimeter of parkland,

patient trees in gardens waiting for someone, an ambulance
paused at the junction. The bus stops. A man,

Her bones passing with time, away from their hold
to museum case or padlocked archive cupboard,

pressed into the after-life as knowledge,
pinned back together by forensic attention,

held from the battering of time's passing;

unlike now, windswept on a high hill,
my hair a struggle of snakes
blown behind the salt sea air
towards my past, laid out across the peninsula —
and my future, deep under its shores.

At Pen Môn

The stones on the beach shift like knots in a charm.
Each crunch a precursor of a spell:

    I find you inside the cairn crouched
            by the patterned stone
                      eyeing the dark.

O Sea, I miss the blue-green heart
of your swell and fall, seal
heat immersed in your wave,
head like a coracle, nose to the cloud.

I miss each step I took along our shoreline
to the lighthouse, old quarry and cave.

Ghosts call to me from over the horizon.

I greet them as friends
as I greet the rise of the hill
and the coitus of the spring and leaf,

all of us running across the headland,

or walking the slope in a storm
or footsteps patterning

I pour my hurt upon you
across all space and time.

The ghosts, they sing –
I hear them in the leaves.

They sing from behind my eyes,
from flesh, from out of me.

The Bones' Lament

O the lovely slicing of the cold
and down into the wet,
down into the emptiness,
a thinning seam of depth.
My knee joints lie like stars
flung out across the bay.
From above I am a map,
a route to guide the way.
'Why drag me back together?'
I whisper to the moon.
'I like being multiple
down here inside the gloom.'
How to leave this watery bed?
I like being calcified.
I like the light as it filters in
and out of the turning tide.
And I like that I'm a tale told
in pubs at closing time.
Why do you need to know
exactly who I am?
What else do you want of me
up there upon the land?

red scarf at the neck like a wound, steps on and shadows follow
from the spooling back streets falling somewhere beneath the wheels;

wooden signposts point to cycle tracks across side roads and on
into deep quickening dusk, rushed love comes in a twilit bed,

a child's eyes spark in the floodlit sports ground and cars circle
the flower-topped roundabout while our old bus warms and hums.

Seafog

    I run to the rain's edge, forgotten
        in the field of drizzle.
            You stood naked
        under the dying tree,
                smiling at me.
The grey encloses us, both without care,
    running down the back roads towards the city's
        ever-lasting light;
                your body unreachable,
    solitary without a gift, broadening
                at the edge of the storm into a cliff face,
                your chest the height of an island cove.

    I cannot climb to you though the wind is high.
    The road is a slip-stream. I am shivering,
        goose-bumped and reddened, cloth-less
            and un-swaddled in a mist, sitting in
    a rowing boat, long red hair streaming behind,
               rowing away, elbows cocked,
                  hot breath,
        a slight sweat, nipples alert
        in the cold night.

I can not land where you are not.
I can not bring the boat to land,

to daylight, rain, wet fog, always here.

One Note

Upstairs my neighbours are singing again,

playing guitar, opening sound to the wind;
the window ajar, rooftops outside lighting

with flecks of voice, brightening
the damp tarmacked alleyway to the bridge,

the fresh fall of leaf, the old school:
a lamp clicks on in an attic room at night;

drums and piano patterning the eaves.
Wet rhythms crumbling through the decades

as cars change colour, or
the newspaper print freshens to new ink:

a child with my eyes
runs across the headland beyond this river

over the ridge to the bus stop at the precinct.
Early morning, she sings open-mouthed

to the sun as it rises along the Welsh hills,
school a dry sentence: the mountains

praised with a loose tune,
a singular love she attaches to the dawn,

to Duck Pond Lane beside the supermarket,
the small brook, dark freckles of light

where the branches reach over the path, always
the risk of silence from behind the trees,

from the shadows which precede the song,
as she flies over wet grass towards the sun.

Congleton Tapestry

Congleton rare, Congleton rare,
Sold the Town Bible to buy a new bear.

A wedding dress weeps as a fiancé sprints away,
top hat bounding the hairline of the hedge;
and through a well-stitched corbelled window,
wide open on the kitchen table, the 1912 Chronicle documents:
'Alleged Breach of Promise in Chester Assizes'
He said they had never walked about the fields together.
He had not met to bring her home from church.
Together the town tuts and cries, then sighs.
And when quietness settles in the lanes,
more flaxen rain. On the High Street
emptiness purrs in the closed-up café
as Anglo-Saxon villagers brew a pot of broth in Priesty Fields
where houses are raised then fall again
like a screen on pause; and as they wait for the decision
of the committee, a line of concerned faces,
warm-hatted, well-booted, peep from behind the hedge,
lever a large wooden wedge which tips the land like a ship at sea.
Towards Astbury Mere a union jack slinks up a flag pole.
A woman in a terraced street tries to wedge new roller blinds
    in her car boot.
In a window box a ginger cat strokes a spider with his arching tail.
And somewhere in 1600 a bear rushes through the

          shopping precinct
pursued by revellers. He expands in the damp Cheshire air,
and a waterfall of rain pours from his giant's fur,
which turns the looms in the factories by the river Dane,
fustian cut to velvet feathers the street with down,
until wet nose at the height of the burial cairn,
the bear slows and bites the edge of the rock,
sharp teeth shaping out the ridge, then turns
and pulses, vanishing into the dusk
where below on the plain, beyond the viaduct, observatory
telescope at an angle to the night like an eye,
the land begins to quake, rock strata
jolt and shake old earth into lucent hills,
rolling slope, glacial lakes. The future waits.

Mossley Hill

On the footbridge lads meet to smoke
with their eyes closed; trains pummel underneath
and beyond them blue summer sky is streaked pink:
fresh wind from the Mersey rustles their shirts.
Down the road in the Chinese a man waits for his order,
the old lady serving speaks in bright Cantonese
and along the alley outside the take-away window
the back-to-backs are face-to-face,
hanging baskets topping in the breeze;
and in my eye-line from the counter to the back of the pub,
lamps flick on in the side bar, footie on the TV,
lovers under the pergola. A couple walk in:
she has pillar-box lips; two lads drink frothy pints
at an iron-legged table, one thumbs a roll-up,
steps outside to savour it as the late sun
rolls across the curve of the hill while
in the allotments at the back of the semis
a man raises a fork which glints as the moon
swollen and ripe, peckers the treetops,
dry mouth folding onto tips of the leaves:
and on the ridge, near the big house, a fire sparks in the woods,
an iron-age hill fort rises from the mulch,
menhir in their padlocked greenhouse
carve spiral patterns onto damp cold rock,
cows ache for the dairy, in the piggery sows give birth;

in the orchard behind the stable-yard
an apple falls to the floor, a child grabs it, runs through a wall
and away into the station where the first trains ran.
A man lies on the track, on blood-sodden gravel,
guard pale-faced, hands cupped around his eyes.
An ambulance soars over the hump of the bridge
like a halo of light; too late tonight,
and in the hedgerow mice seep into shadow,
scramble through fencing; a cat sleeps on the far wall.

High Tide
A lyric

    Sail me, city, to heavens below.
    Sail me, city, into depths of dark.
    Sail me, city, into the hook of the estuary.
    Sail me, city, to the clutch of the heart,

    onto the high seas, under surfaces
    through sunken shadow from old oil-lit shores
    to the feline jaw of a tidal swish
    and the bright-eyed bite of the cormorant.

    I want the wild wet and the long depths,
    strong undertow and tidal concerns,
    but the harbour lights are drawing me in:
    I fear dry land, sandbanks and stone.

    Sail me, city, to heavens below,
    Sail me, city, into depths of dark.
    Sail me, city, into the hook of the estuary.
    Sail me, city, to the clutch of the heart.

    Onto the high sea, under surfaces
    through sunken shadow from the old oil-lit shore
    to the feline jaw of the tidal swish
    and the bright-eyed bite of the cormorant.

O sail me, city, into the filth of the storm.
Bring the salt from my pores; let my eyes colour dawn.
O city, sail me away from settled land
into ocean's wreck and rough; back into love.

Please do not leave me earthbound.
Please do not leave me earthbound.

a careful tread around the silent church.

I light a candle for our passing
                        and watch it burn.

                    *

I carry you with me
                        each day out of the dark.

And today is about salt-traces,
the memory of darkness, of the ritual and the aftermath,
mound in the dark trees:
    an oxen burial by three entry stones.

We eat our picnic on the vantage point
and watch the rooks
    swing down, down to the copse.

And my half-immersion in your tide
                        haunts my skin;
half my shins salted and given to your wave.
The rest of me scalded by the sun
loitering somewhere
undone and fuzzy at the edges of the land.

A child hides behind

fir trees; a young woman
lies in the long grass behind the wall.

You and me in the woods, hand in hand.
You take a picture. The hills frame the sky.

I try to write you over and over
but still I cannot say what you are.

        Woman.

You run down the lane towards the sea.
Your hands turning to skin,
waxy and folding in.

I can see you, shadow self,
shod in mud, moving across
    the stones to the beach with an ease as if
        you cannot feel them shift and
           cut beneath your soles —
rubbing smooth each corner of a future,
as you are shifting, feet to flippers
   and eyes to the horizon.
     You hear a song sung to the wind
     and peer in and under,
        until fully seal again, you bob and swim
     turning to watch three women

       picnicking on the ridge,
        watching your head perk-up,
totemic in the blue,
their open mouths calling:
Come back to us, come back.

from **THE WELL AT WINTER SOLSTICE**
(2019)

St Seiriol's Well

Midnight

A half-dressed man is sitting on the ledge
in a small hut, mortar-clad and damp with dew,
his knees folded to his chest, long hair as white
as the light which floods the grass;
each stalk bright like a lightning-struck tree.

And he is waiting for me to come and look
but I am still staring over the wall.
He has huge silver eyes like pools.
He is the pool, now a man
sat waiting to hold me,
to put his wet fingers around my waist

and I want to go to him
but I am also in the stream,
in the small brook which feeds the sea.

I am bare-foot and wearing only white
and the night is brittle cold and there is no-one else
apart from the moon
that glistens as I glisten

for I am the moon.

I am the reflection on the water as it runs,
sequential, down towards the sea.

I am a ripple, I am a wave
moving out into the sticky blue,
flattening and thinning – diffusing
like light, mixing with the swell
to form a deep swollen shadow;

and he is throwing copper pennies into the well,
which cascades waves like feathers over skin.

And he is walking to the stile
and the white limestone walls
and then he is not there at all,
never has been and I am now reeling,
coiling, the moon above is who I am
trickling down to the sea, to the sea.

Cool, crystal light within each gesture.
Clean and clear is my thought.
Crisp and horizontal is my action.

Two silver ovals shimmer back from my surfaces.
I thin outwards into the water

fully-lost and fully-formed.

Dawn

And I am a fish in the pond low near the rushes.
And I am in the branches of the trees in the high bird song.
And I am in the church tower leaning on the bell.
And I am in the grass as the trowel rips through.
And I am in the water as it strains through earth to the sea.
And I am in the thin heat of the April sun.

And he has gone in the daylight
back into the stone,
a body laid into the limestone dusted with moss.
He faces into the stone and watches the dark.

For he only shines when the moon
is full, for he is the moon,
the moon in the rock,
a fallen moon
rolling out from the source
and into the night,

a grounded moon,
a dry-landed moon

lying on the shore like an upturned ship.

Dusk

Psalms seep out from the priory like a whisper
as monks slice mackerel on wooden plates and hear
only the waves, the only constant, that rock
and hold them through the dark-filled night
and Seiriol in his sheepskin turns away from
the wind but speaks slowly to the trees
that swing and sing a soft harmony as birds
scratch their busy tunes into the sky;
and a woman in a purple raincoat
walks towards the well, a yellow ribbon
stained red dangles on the brambles
as the spring jangles its journey over rocks and away
and the woman reaches her pale fingers into the water,
swirls it around, puts the liquid to her lips,
slight-salt, iron-tang, and disappears
like vapour, like a splinter
and down into the rock like an axe
and down into the sea like a fish
and down into the soil like embers in a fire pit
where the bones of a lamb burn bright
and down, holding the lamb in her arms,
and down and out together, past the quarry, past the graveyard,
and the lamb has a child's face then a lamb's face
as they all unravel like the threads in her jumper
tumbling under and down, down into the earth.

Bridie's Tomb
August 2016, St James Cemetery, Liverpool

    The pall-bearers balance on the wet grass,
    finding their footing as the coffin
    is carried along the slope towards the well.
    The only well in Liverpool which can heal the dead,
    I've heard it said by the dead
    who laugh and giggle behind the graves.

    Sea-wind flings itself over the city
    full-heartedly in a wide embrace.
    Figures walk towards the mausoleum and then disappear.
    Sun settles a little then runs into the cloud.
    Children died. Five years. One. Gone.
    The curl of the clock wrings the day dark.

    'Hold still,' she says. 'Let me feel your pulse.'
    I let her grab my wrist, thumb
    my jugular, listen to the space
    blood runs warm. Her eyes smile.
    She sighs. 'Listen for us. The rough of
    the walk; all hurt is hunger.'
    A drum. Then a gull. Car on the road.

    Stopping at the spring, the bearers
    sip a drop and each sprout

wings from their shoulders. Feathered
white plumage, lift-on-up,
reheard as gulls squall on the salt.

'Be here,' she says. 'Be as sure as you can,
deep in the meld of your days.
Mine passed like waves, brocade
and parlours, distant view from the window
of the ships in the dock, unloading their
cargo. Father said not to look.
No. No-one said to see it all. We learnt
this after our house was
bought with the proceeds of others' pain.'

'How much of your life,' she says
turning to me white eyes alight,
'is balanced on the unseen,
scratched deep, long nights avoiding
sweats brought about by the shadows?
Or the bold extravagance of not caring,
of not being able. Are you able?'

She catches my arm, holds it up to the light.
A garnet ring shimmers in the afternoon sun.
'You are nearly undone. You hear us speak.'
I call out, 'Speak what?' 'Just listen,' she replies
'to what is out of sight, the closed room deals

and the casino nights. Listen to the men
as they make their pacts;
you might be part of an agreement, just like me.'

'He took me to the sea,' one girl says.
'I was sold to the night,' cries another
as she throws her arms around a tomb.
'I was whipped later. Never free.'
'I died of cholera, dysentery. No clean water.'

'Write what you hear, poet, or we will disappear.'

St James's at Dusk

Today the light is as faded as the sound
of the street above the cemetery.
A crow caws on its flight above our heads,
over the weight of bodies leaning into the dusk
until all of us are sinking in the rush of the afternoon.
A couple seen at the bus-stop, fresh from the train,
walk past again holding hands – we are still to meet.
And somewhere in the mush
freshly wrought beginnings rustle in their sleep,
dust off the damp of their winter coats, shake
plumes of curly hair and flushed cheeks,
walk along the track back up towards the mausoleum,
sandstone glowing gold as the sun sets
over the Welsh mountains'
burning snowy tops, light spooling out and across
the rocks which spin the red heat
like the hands of a clock.

Passage Grave

Inside the chamber each pattern is alight
as a strip of sun seeks damp shadow
within chiselled grooves to swirl the bright into black.

The light, deep inside the dark,
finds new routes across the rock.
Each grain of sandstone is compressed time,
a salty fleck in a watery suspension,

moving within and across the solid matter
to restart and renew its shift into shadow.
The shadow becomes lit and the light
becomes dark.

The stone is not inert
but processing the darkness, turning it back into
light, light turning back into dark,

as years spiral onwards and into the rain,
prescient on the horizon,

grey cloud about to burst with this moment
woven and weaving one day to the next.

Song Cycle

Imbolc

I want to stay in the weather,
within the feel of the rain,
within the soft call of the wind,
within the light on the sand.

I want to stay in the weather,
inside the curve of the sky and call of the birds.
I want to stay in the weather,
inside the whole of the light,
inside the touch of the day.

I am a fall of leaves,
a crisp under-foot layer of mulched-down matter.
To turn into the city is to turn to brick.
How heavy that is.
How hard to shift.

Beltane

I am the flow of your blood
and the touch of the moon.
I am your love boiling over on a summer's day.
I am your heart burnt by too much sunlight.
I am your laughter crumbling into the long grass.

O little lover –
you are my heart and the flower of me.
I pitch out into the May Day air.
I am at the centre of it all as I fall
into you, bloom, and back into stars
and sweat. I am at the centre of it all –
sad-faced on an empty street
or in the moon-lit park
or in the alley that leads to the bridge.

Let me go. Let the heat go south for the winter.
Am I not here? I am everywhere
and you are within me, every stroke of my hair,
eyelash blink, flat-line of your eye.
I am everywhere and O I am not.

Lughnasadh

Under the trees light is a tissue,
layers stuck to layers, light upon light.
I peel it back slowly to see what hides
long and wet in the deep shadow,
flattened out and moulding in the summer air.

A stare – an eye looks back up from the mud.
One large green baleful eye blinks, closes,
opens like a cloud passing away from the sun.
I use my fingers to remove the earth.
From the rest of the head a nose protrudes,
a mouth opens, breath like a gale
pulling me into the swell of the shadow.

I cannot see the sunlight, the trees
lean in and cover me with their branches
like a swaddled child. Here in the glade
behind the old oaks the head shakes
grains of soil from its skin,
seems to settle, keeps staring
up at the sky, caught behind the green,
long eyelashes like new shoots
flicker in the spray of soil flung
from my hands' rough digging, scraping
at the edges to carve out a space to see.

There is no body, just this face in the mulch
watching the trees grow, watching time pass.

I have to keep the vision clear.

When the snow comes I melt the frost.
When the dry winds crack the mud
I scrape away the dust.
When the leaves fall I shift the slurry
with these hands. I see the changes
that time cannot. I need eyes to mark
the distance beyond these gnarly trunks.

A fox runs in the long grass.
I hear him howl. He catches the sun in his tail.

He meant to catch the moon.

Now he runs away with the stars
which are not the only light in his eyes –
burning orange fur, a fire screeching
across the landscape like a comet.

Samhain

When the dark came
I was sleeping. He knocked at the door
in the middle of the night.
I let him in while dreaming.
He saw all my fear, all my fright
cornered like a lamplit hare.
Shivering, he was a green man
and I was a ghost.
The night walked across the threshold
and the seed was laid
beneath the corridor, roots like algal bloom
swelled in the air and carried me to you —

O love you are a river.
I am full of silt.
I want the world to ache,
to feel this throbbing
as the evening falls, exhausted,
across the woodland floor.

My love is like a footstep
quiet on the earth, unheard
until I wake you from
shelter in the dry lands
beyond the restive tide.

In Midsummer

A woman running through the shrubbery,
straight ahead through the rhododendron bush.
She has bare legs, a long shirt, bare feet,
runs as if the foliage isn't there,
running from something that follows her.
But there is nothing. No body comes.
Where is she going?
Here she is again. She turns, looks behind,
long blonde hair blown back.
For her it is night, I can see that –
and it has been raining. For me, it is heat
and a June-basked day in the glade
that works my sense – head to the left,
swift twitch to the right.
Here she comes again, on the same track
which isn't a track, a desire path
between conifers trips across her route.
She flits over wheatgrass, saplings
slimed with snail-drawn rivers.
What comes after her from the shade
between the silver birch? Beyond,
white of daisies on the lawn-green.
She runs from the right out of the sunlight,
appears – here she is again – from behind
the patina of holly leaves like woodblock

print against the sun. And then still in front of me,
her bare legs lean over where I sit on grass.
She turns her head, looks back,
looks forward, runs on, skims the purple
just-gone-over rhododendrons. I turn
to see her curve into the shadow
where leaf is bold and covers all
definition. And as my spine
twists on its pelvis, there she is again,
– who will break this? My
observation of her gesture keeps her looped
in the woodland glade forever. Where do I go?
How do I leave? A rustle in the trees,
blackbird hunting for grubs.

The Well at Winter Solstice

Water sucks light slipt between trees,
moon opening out of the cloud
and under the cover of a slanted roof,
a flat black square edged with slate,
walls wet redbrick porous and sodden;
and across the lane, one-light-on,
a cottage at an angle to the earth
watches mountains across the straits,
car headlights scanning the seashore
like eyes reading ink; and he is here —
a foot on wet stone, marking the mass,
crushing life from lichen slipped down
into shallows, absorbed into darkness
that is his thighs, muscular legs rising
like a seal in the ocean after the hunt;
his skin drips with ink, the ink pool
stains grey moon-bit stone and he walks,
has a torso upon a lithe pelvis, steps
onto a ledge and bends low to be seen
by the shadow, held under the shadow
pressing onto his shoulders like a gale;
and in his nakedness, his night-lit watery cobalt,
he steps onto the grass and towards me
standing under the tree; he does not see me
for I am wall and bark and stone and moss:

I see with their eyes as he treads
heavy blue-black onto winter-cut grass
and gravel rolls under each step, sharp
clicks to smooth and the tree branch tip
flicks with a change in air-pressure,
as the stream eyes him like an eclipse
high above its flow, his liquid hair at his waist;
he wades across crushed stones,
and down through me, unseen, in his way.
I close my eyes and the night is blank,
my mind submerged in pigmented depth.
I fall out of this temporary self,
his tune in my mouth wet and warm
forms long notes of an ancient song,
a chant I do not know. My lips taste salt,
and his voice is deep ground,
sung like cattle low across empty fields
and a rustle in the openness
as he reveals the graves, the church beyond
which is listening and the stone cross
behind the screen in the dark
startles and hears me, hears us sing
out across the sea; the patterns re-ravel,
the water in my voice swollen
with the lick of his steps, heavy, certain,
down the signposted track to the car park,
past the hut and the sleeping cat,

past the barred gate and the cows in their barn,
past the twine, tyres, feed,
plastic wrap, new laid posts
and into the quarry and into the sea
and under the sea into the tide
and into the tide, into the cave
at the ocean bed where mountains
root like teeth into soft sand
and into the end of the light
where no moon slips within
and no words are heard or visions seen.
In the cave, I swim in him and him in me
and we come to be like we began,
silence speaking as loudly as he can.
Listen: he talks of a river with a rocky shore
and a woman bobbing in the water,
her face smiles to the sky, dreams
of long beaches, sea creatures
and sunsets over the sea-salty estuary,
of the far ocean and the deep return
as we crawl ashore on hands and knees,
our skin on sharp sand grazed pink,
sticky grit, cold tight on bare backs,
to where shingle turns to bramble –
standing at last, naked, walking steady
through the quarry and through the farm
towards the cottage and the light,

towards the stream and freshwater,
towards the well at winter solstice,
along the path towards the pond
under the gateway built of limestone,
where he leans now on the far side
in shadow, his hair blows like ivy blows
as if he doesn't have to travel anywhere today
but will rest and watch the blue sky turn grey
and the light slide away into the year,
watch as I pace up new-laid path
pulling shrivelled blackberries from the bush;
then I am there at night, shaken in the dark,
then there at dawn, cold in reluctant light,
then there or next year, another solstice,
my steps, sticky slow on a summer's day
or a sodden run through fresh fallen rain.
Still the spring stream disappears, unseen
into folds of leathery green, as snow
arrives out of the distance, sun
burrows into many horizons,
rays like bells ringing out of the soil.
And then stillness at the well but weighted
down, not a swim in deep water
but a shallow dive through to find
the basin bottom where copper pennies
lie like wreckage or many fallen suns.
I lower myself into the cold, squat,

avoid sharp stones on my soles,
and my body collapses like the skin it is;
all bone and blood pools into the well.
I am fluted, folded over like a cloth.
And in the rectangle of the entrance, framed
walking up the path, he has been to the shore,
trails seaweed behind each step like tentacles,
puts his hand into water, into me,
swirls the pool like wind in a tree.
Within the flow, feel how the spring,
so slow circles, churns over in a spin.
I am a sea-otter coiling somersaults
as he washes fresh salt into this bath of me,
turns and lies on wet grass like a tired dog
and from across the coast, dense sea fog,
a diesel engine hiss stills at a distant jetty;
one slant of thin sun slips into the mud.
There is no speech here pushing through;
the clear liquid now puddled with me
becomes inkier, loaded with deposits,
like a rock turning over in the tides
left to soak in flows from beyond my grasp:
an owl balanced on the branch, shut-eyed;
a rat in dark rivulets scurries through.
A bat overhead curves back as dusk
sinks again; always the day is lost
as I wash away one inscription

and listen for the next. And when
my body reappears as snow, as raven,
as tree, as fish, as hillside, as reflection on the pond,
as reed bed cut low for winter,
as pine needles on a gravel path,
as sun over the horizon from the next day,
as sea-wind miles inland softens the skin,
I pull myself up out of the water,
shake her down, dry her in the wind.
Sharp sky picks through the distance,
starlings rise at speed above my head.
Heart-beat, breath, gull-cry, rain-soon
sounds in my skin, mud catches toes.
He stands and drips sea-salt, all light,
down into the well, dampness glows.
A voice calls my name. I know the sound.
A light in the cottage beats on, then off.
And I look out from the kitchen window
at mountains framed by white flaking paint;
behind, two children at a low table,
faces caught in the hands of the moon.
They just sit static, painted-on,
and the night stares hard, watches
to see how I move towards them
as if they are real children. Outside,
a man and a women shuttle along,
seem to be sodden, seen to be caught in the rain,

but there is no rain, just the reign of the moon
and a man standing at an open door.
He arrives in a raincoat every evening
but he has only been to the shore
from where he drops a tide of pebbles
on the threshold and shakes silt
out from his hair; as the door closes
he becomes the raincloud that he is
and all I see through the streaky pane
is his face shift from man into wave,
pour like a waterfall over the gorse.
And the rain on the roof is my relation,
also dripping down inside the well,
and he comes again over the ocean,
in from the cave in the shape of a storm
as the brickwork turns its inside to the wind,
and outside I turn and the cottage
is stone-dark-blue, no one-light-on,
just tree-shadowed curve to the fence,
and he is sat on a wall on the headland,
back-turned, and he is stood at my side
as if he is my shadow long laid into dark.
The sea slops at the jetty over the rise
as we travel along the stony path,
towards the empty well where he bends
all swollen whole of his liquid self,
dives head first back into the basin,

and I smooth into sleet and high wind
across open sea, all the flush of me
in a strong hold, pushing my spine,
bending my back over into a wave,
speaking into my ears with a cold that pierces,
for my eyes to look through to see the way,
for this mouth to call out to gravity and all force,
for my hands to snap and break to fling,
to take part in the erosion and I am willing,
I can hear it asking in each gesture,
pummelling of pressure; and I cup my hand
and drink him in, my tongue and gullet
flushed with liquid scooped from the well.
Water shines through my bones like glass,
like a sun through cloud it streams
between my legs, out from my mouth,
from my hair which is also water,
rivers of it, waves splash across a forehead
of rain clouds and midwinter mist,
a haze of sea-salted air blooms and blows
as my belly and eyes flood and gush,
palms dip to hold then still again;
and strewn across the winter grass,
over the well-stream which runs to the sea
and into the woods, downy feathers;
and in the undergrowth, a pigeon
red-belly and taloned legs facing the sky.

All the coins have been taken from the well.
A stray penny lies on the wet stone.
In an alcove, two twigs bound with dried grass
and a red candle burnt down low.

Keeping the Doors Open

Why should the modern displace the ancient,
around which cluster so many sacred associations?
—Rev. W.D. Wood Rees, A History of Barmby Moor, 1911

    Light on a bay roof, slither of sun across a lawn,
    a mammoth's tooth on the leather-lined table,
    dust on a pile of papers by the window, beyond
    a garden, camellia crisp with ice
    and row of fir trees line a mossy sandstone wall;
    black wrought-iron gate open to the road
    and across the country lane a redbrick boundary
    and then the parish church of Barmby Moor,
    stained-glass window high above the cemetery
    where a figure stands, white collar at his throat,
    a long wool cassock to the uncut grass,
    and he waves with one hand towards the porch,
    walking ahead of me one step at a time.
    He turns inside, under the carved wood mantle
    and pauses at the doorway, as I do.
    Inside is a different church, back in Llanrhidian,
    January sun seeps through dimpled glass
    as at the altar stands another man in vestments
    who holds high a chalice, passing communion
    to parishioners, kneeling, invisibly, at the step.
    Behind me, in the porch, a lamp catches on,

a lamp no-longer there, shines as if lit for the first time
and a quick woman's voice and three men talk
beyond the walls. Their footsteps tap away
along the path and I look towards the altar
and the priest is walking down the aisle, inscrutable,
an eye to a hand held out from the front row,
and as he reaches the space in front of my breath,
this cold inwards air, he thins, disperses; in one gulp
I draw him in, breathing my self back into the light.
A knock at the door of the closed porch. The light is off,
the light has gone. I walk in from a bright summer's day,
stay still, can't move, locked in the transition,
then disintegrate, coil, find myself, finger-in-the-soil,
curling back ivy for a name carved on long-eroded stone,
grit of dried earth under my nails, a moment
inside the grave, laid quiet in the still of the coffin,
then wormed through the body of a yew
whose trunk sinks into my torso like a last breath,
then flat and thinned, long and lean, crawling
along its branches, an ear to the estuary in the distance;
a drum sounds from the limestone outcrop below,
and the church is a cliff-face and the marsh is a sea
and the beat throbs; and songs are sung later
in the church hall; – comic, music-hall, a ballad –
notes turned to one register I reach into and I am gone.

from **TAM LIN OF THE WINTER PARK**
(2022)

Portent in the High Woods

The men sit before the hearth,
spit words into flames. Some thing
is coming over the mountains,
along forest tracks and past the stream.

They know this as he saw it in a dream,
heard horses' hooves stick in sandy mud,
saw in his sleep a shadow in the high wood,
long-lined like a tree but swerving
down the path like a torrent.

He says this out loud. Men lean inwards,
look east across lead-lined windows,
terraced gardens, sodden topiary
to feathery fog, the flood.

And in woods, at a fire-pit
in the grove, twigs are laid on the centre-stone,
a mist swirls then scatters
as oaks creak and crack, cloudy droplets
skulk like rainclouds over the earth.

At their hearth, the men cackle,
scramble for spears and swords.
Across mountains, in the estuary,
the thick tide is far and out.
Lithe winds ride in over the valley.
One man licks his lips to taste the salt.

*

In the grove, weary bodies rest
on the sound of the mist, which crunches
now like the rock that it is or was
before it came to be lost here at the tip
of the sky. And the stone underneath
their bones rustles, glitters, sand
shifts apart granite, then particles
smack on particles, eroding
pleasurably into strata. Muscles
ache as they dream, bone on sinew,
clench and pull, scratch at nerve endings,
stretch out ligaments; worn down, they sleep.

*

The men creep beneath the trees,
torches held high under drips
from the moss. At the end
of the path, a pant like a dog,
a sea-wind, then fog hung

in the old oak grove as,
like foxes from a hole, they
reach the fire-pit, poke it till it burns
bold and mist-borne breath
shines bright like constellations

and there are no bodies sleeping,
only piles of sticks and stones
lain in the shape of a human
lost in the twine of time and rot.

*

When morning comes, the men sit at the embers of the fire.

In the ash, a drawing of a body of a man.

In their eyes, silence –
    like they never began
        to chase away the salted air
           blown over the valley from the lips of the sea.

A curlew cry on a newly-wetted beach;
a spoken song, words born of mist, not ink.

Tam Lin of the Winter Park

You walk ahead of me, beckoning, disappearing.
You open the side of a tree, step through bark
to another park, which is a series of rooms

laid out on leaf mulch, and on a sofa,
near a sycamore, you lean on upholstery,
smiling, gesturing, opening your arms,

then turn your back as I step into the glade;
muscular branches lean and block my way
as I stop to see you, still grinning, still watching,

asking, 'O how will you get in?' A chimney
puffs. Bricks are built with grey. I peer in
while you stare through a shining window.

'Come in,' you say, 'Come in,' but when I
place my palm on the handle, I push into air,

and you are calling, not unkindly, 'O do come in,'

as I search in the leaves for a key, to solidify
walls, to make the barrier more convincing.

Escape at Red Rocks

I am the colour of the outside,
a stillness moving like a winter tide,
a new shoreline in formation,
a marshland waterlogged – soggy
ground needs time to dry it out –

but time as sea wind not calendar, the time
found inside spaces stretching out and over
like skin on a drum is a resonance,
a wave that submerges the entire rock,
not chiselling or scratching at one area only,
not just a mind to impress upon

but a flattened and silken self
all bound into the support of the water,
head rising up then down to find my breath.

Peregrine

Falcons by the belfry slide across a square of blue
between the sandstone tower and spring-green trees,

triangular wings fixed realities against currents
supporting each journey over the twitchers' cameras.

Below, feathers lie along the tarmac
like the after-math of a drunken party

and in the porch a pigeon hunches to warm a nest
behind a row of thin steel pins

lining a noticeboard's dark wood rim. Posters
invite attendance at the Easter services.

And on a sandstone ledge, her mate perches, plump and grey,
eyes me, nods. I walk in, light widening from gable windows

and like a field of roses in bloom viewed from a hill above the valley
pigeons line polished pews, each warm body sat close to another.

At the altar, no cross but more feathers
and an egg on a silver platter; the gods of the sky

call like a round of thunder and all the birds ascend,
falcons to the sun and pigeons to the rafters

as the day outside the window still does not blossom with rain.

By the Walled Garden

The heaviness fell into my arms, resisted,
as I tried to move into another shape,

like the weight it is, carried in my muscles'
salt, blood and gravity; daylight pinned

beneath the cloud – sometimes sharp,
sometimes kind – as I am bound to this spot,

turning my torso to receive the salted air.

O my ocean, do you still rush against the shore?
To be in you, to be sea-shorn, sea-blown,

wide, so wide, so wide, I cannot be lost.

Old House

Gone, it stands only as a shadow, a ghost
of itself, pulsing in the sun. Inside
its transparent body, a tree, a stone cairn.
Sun burnishes fires outside wooden huts.

>*Blow through this, sea-gust.*
>*Come inside, stay with us.*

And bright as the earth's red crust,
the flames push through this thin place
on the ridge as impressions of people
stride across the heat and do not burn.

>*Blow through this, sea-gust.*
>*Come inside, stay with us.*

The figures are from later and see only
furnished rooms where thin-robed
women stare down from walls into coals
bright in the fireplace; a winter's day,

>*Blow through this, sea-gust.*
>*Come inside, stay with us.*

not July, heavy, soot-soaked rain
down-river from the city sticks to the glass,
whilst from the north window daylight
beats across the carpeted floor like a snake.

> *Blow through this, sea-gust.*
> *Come inside, stay with us.*

And the garden blooms with bursts of foamy
murmuration of rose and wildflower
which root within the hill like songs
playing out from a choir of voices

> *Blow through this, sea-gust.*
> *Come inside, stay with us.*

and the house is throbbing and can be undone
with a squint of the eye and the lash of the wind
or the door is a wolf and is a mouth
lined with teeth that bite onto time as it falls into the hall

> *Blow through this, sea-gust.*
> *Come inside, stay with us.*

amongst the bricks; time as a full breath by a beating chest.
And the house balloons on the breeze,
rainbow-threaded and oily-sheened,
floats over the oak tree and out to sea.

> *Blow through this, sea-gust.*
> *Come inside, stay with us.*

Mothballed
IM Marsh Campus, Bark Hill House

Scraps of white paint fleck redbrick steps, guano
spots the concrete under the veranda, behind my back,
French doors to the hallway, classroom chairs.

But turning west, I look up and over, past the salt
grit box on the sloping track from studio to gym,
the river long, so sharp, shining; wintery branches

wind-whipped, pirouette; sun, global, sways over
dark-paned accommodation blocks.
Spherical streetlamps light every evening for no-one

coming home to this faded mansion. Inside,
at a cracked window, his wife notes again the elegant line
of the water, the sublime Welsh hills, drinking tea in perpetuity

as over damp-stained streaky woodchip magnolia
slither visions of plantations, tropical sunsets, blood.

Brân in Harlech

The sea in a gale crushes the barnacles.
Battlements rumble in the shift of the rain.

A man the size of a cargo ship clambers
out of the ocean, a land-locked whale,
and his head at the neck is slit
by a volley of knives swung like silence
across a room as his bone splits
against another push of thunder.
Blood is a baby seal, a frightened child.

His head bobs like a pup or seaweed
on the white froth, now a strong pink –
and is floated inland, rowed ashore with care
to prop up the rocks, to stop the flow,

to compress the wounds of all those who died.

Divination at High Water

Small birds dip on the tide,
one instant silver, next dark as shadow
and, seep-into-it, disappear again
in the glint of sun on the wave;
and turning under into the crust of water,
taking on edges and then reversing, then — flicker —

there is no need to carry
a narrative high on my shoulders
as the light makes me another story,
touching distance huge as the earth's arc,

no collapse of form or dissolution, but an alteration,
a submission to the sky and then, for a moment,
enlarged as wide as a firmament,
my body, a long afternoon of rain, becomes thunder.

Turned Earth

Down, down rots leaf to beetle and fungi.

The rusted iron railings that edge the park
are coppery green reminders of definition

as cut clods lean up on an elbow
like a body in a bed, and raise a loamy
face to my gaze, exhale a hilly breath, pick
up handfuls of mulch, munch gravelly
mouthfuls, then as a dog barks
in the beyond just past the parkland gates,
lean over and settle back onto felty
deep-dug, claggy cushions, seep
under into spade-cut humps and muck

as the allotments lie fallow, forgetting us.

Five Breaths
(2024)

Five Breaths

were needed to extinguish the flame
and now a red wick leans into the melt,

diving into a quarried lake
high in the mountains to find mouthfuls
of salt in the freshwater under the slate.

Here, dust edges the decorations.

The holly wreath curls, browns,
is a woodland floor alongside a stream
which pours towards the quarry.

Inside the wreath berries are the eyes of a fox
on the grass verge along the back lane
which runs towards the Hill.

*

2 am; I hear them in the dark
of the spare room the day after Christmas,
a scream like a child being hit

and then a long extension
like the downstroke of a comma
hangs in the air and repeats five times

as they patrol along the markings
of the side streets, stepping pawprints over the double yellow,
disappearing into alleys to return and process

towards the cemetery across Boundary Road
where a candle burns in a derelict chapel,
(funds are sought for its repair),

and the fox with the red hair and human face,
leans across the municipal railings
and towards the chancel, then blows

through canine teeth, five times,
as the light waivers but will not go out.

Quarried Stone

Letters erode as I rub a finger in the cut,
M, D, O, once engraved onto ochre-red rock;
and crusted with sand and plumped with blood,
my cheeks face the wind's straight flight to the crag.

I nestle into this overhang, grains bite on cotton,
beaching on my forehead, in my matted hair,
and like slate is spliced to tile a roof I split,
fold away from my feet, carry the weight

of my leaning as I tip back, open mouth wide to grit,
fall backwards into hillside strata. In each era
I lick, eat, absorb the stone, wrap arms tight
within the matter, then land as an outline of a creature

daubed onto a cave wall with soot from a fire.
O I can't be held or seen, now I am sand and stone.

In the Woods at Caerdeon

Cadair Idris lies under the cloud line,
slumbering under a weight of moss
and vertical rain which does not reach

the inside of me, to sink sodden into my thought –
but turns and walks, in a trajectory,
on stilts almost, towards the sea

who has all of us here, rain, human, moss,
in its eye, staring back inside our perception
as the mountain shifts on its haunches,

scales shimmering with the same rain
which falls through the rock-lined
lives of the stream in front of my boots.

So, I am a spider-web between all edges –

and conker-brown leaves flip over in the wind
and a light appears on the path up the hill

and a figure there on the stretch to the top,
at night swings a lantern to see me
here in the shadows, haunting them still.

The Hill

At night, I hear it calling,
leaves rattle on the silver birch bark,
remembering itself to me
as I turn to sleep in this terrace house
as the storm slants past the window
to keep me here and in bed tonight.

At the far end of the memorial gardens
at the foot of the hill is a woodland walk,
darkened now a few days after full moon,
light spans the branches across the railings,
across the back of the new-build rooftops,
across the Moss and straight then towards the sea

who wells there murmuring also of the trees.
We are here. We are here. And the rain falls.

The Cat is at the Back Door

watching the night as the blue-bright-black
folds across the brick wall backs

dignified by the covering of dark,
shaped to suggest their mass and
thrust up towards the remaining pool of sky.

Voices on the street.

From the box room I can hear
a love song through the plaster
to sooth across the long night

where we lie eyes open in our beds
waiting for love which comes and goes

as it always should, aching into us with a precision
as bright as the strip of blue across the chimneys.

O love, I wait into the air as it covers us.

What else is there in the crumbling dusk
to hold our hearts to and say this is real
when worldly tasks fail to secure the time?

Commute

Over the heavens we go, and the streets
roll down, thundering under

my step as I walk from the bus
down past the terrace

which whips to the sea
houses riding on snaking tarmac.

The road mirrors the Hill
peaking upwards into summit

then cupping down
into sandstone moons

hung in a ring around its neck.

*

The city has extracted me –
thrown me back over the water
or under it always into
tug and pull of river
which hangs above the tunnel
roof, lips lining along

the sandstone bed. How great
is his tongue, lonely Mersey
falling over always into the rock's
watery sheen I pour under.

*

The town has a fur in this heat,
a pink shimmer -
In and out we go, rolling
through the evening, into
the air and out of it,
into squeeze of bubbles blistering
as cars roll through their force.

The town is settling in.
The river unseen flows unheard.
The windmill is atop the Hill. Always.
Three sails patched against the haze.

In Birchen Head

The far side of the hill is where the wind rests,
come past the lighthouse, across the Moss,

unhindered by landfill and rewilded pools
to where a giant lies prostrate alert to the sea, palms

outstretched cupping the marsh, fingertips are promontories,
his back, the heathland scrub then the woodland crest

where the big houses catch a view to Liverpool,
cathedrals, warehouses; town hall clock face

hovers above treetops in the park. A heart beats
inside sandstone, ripples within the rock. Eyes

witness clouds shifting formation as grey turns to white
and the red light of a plane trails across the dawn.

The hill is awakening. The hill is always awake,
listening to car ignitions as we start early to work.

Artificial trees in bay windows glimmer, and outside later,
the charity float is a Mari Lwyd, collection buckets

rattling from door to door, lights
shimmering for children to eye and sparkle; more rain.

The giant blinks as night calls in again.

*

The house is charmed and lit for solstice.
It holds light and life. A cat sings in the dark of the window,

a living space, blessed with shine within the dark
which surrounds and cocoons,

swaddles its watchful face in a shadow until dawn
always looking at the street. The patterns of the day-to-day

here lilt and whistle, lighting a power amongst dereliction
and crumbling concrete yards a mile from here, the river

once a tidal pool, corralled into dockyards where grey sheds
and metal fencing cast shadows across the tarmac

and the water clings to the mossy steps
of the sandstone slabs which hold erosion in place

whispering a moon-blown word across fresh surfaces,
taking the small stony particles into the belly

as the ferry berths and cars roll off
and the grasses in the cracks of the cobbles

by the quay sway in a breeze. O wounded headland, -

and all want an engine, a mechanism, a use.

Summer Solstice in Callister Gardens

If a sanctuary is a meeting place,
a gift beneath the sky,

then these old brick walls can hold
all the force of wild spring,

all seeds borne beyond and over
the wrought-iron gates to sprout and bloom

in the warming earth to lessen
weary limbs, tired minds,

after the storm and volt of winter
passes into germination, heat crackles on skins.

A cut across the crust of a seed,
freed then falls into itself and the burning dark.

*

Inside dark earth, a shudder of sprig and bud
rise to wet and pallid skies. Brick walls weighty

with moss and rain, watch over as hands dig
into enveloping soil, the fingers are glaciers,
scraping new mountains beneath the strawberries

as the grass is shorn, a spread and curl of sound,
as a brick arch is built by hand, a threshold,
as a vegetable patch is turned with foot and fork

a fleet of seeds sail on the wind,
and back into the street, where a woman reads a name
on a wrought-iron gate; cars drone —

and flushed with feathers looking down from atop the wall,
I see a man standing silent in the centre of the solstice night,
his wife and daughter lost to fever a hundred years ago

as lamps go out for bed in the windows of new houses,
he has a force ratcheting through his body like a charge
shorting down his spine and into the ground,

into a fork resting in the greenhouse, shakes awake,
a glint of silver on its three stuck prongs
as he tends the herbs in the night-filled garden,
then again at dawn rots down into rose, peony, vine.

Bidston Hall on Sunday Afternoon

Beside the stone wall at the edge of the wood,
stepping down on a bramble scratching at my ankle
I stood silently, you behind on the gravel,
me watching a muddy field for any sign of trespass,

and after this, after tracking back along the sandstone ridge,
our many-eyed hill scanning the sky,
past the Observatory, lighthouse, windmill,
through Taylor's wood; and, after, at full moon,

I close my lids to see again what else was in the field,
a tracing I could not see inside thin winter sun,
three or four steps tread on rain-drenched pasture
and a figure walks where now there are no fences,
only stones unclaimed by moss and a grey mare grazing.

All is then redden-gold, and each glint and shimmer
echoes my gut's turn at the almost sting of the thorn
as you waited on the path for me to find my way out of time.

Acknowledgements

Feeding Fire was first published by Spout in 2001. *Andraste's Hair* was first published by Salt in 2007. *Eliza and the Bear* was first published by Salt in 2010. *Arne's Progress* was first published by Arne Press in 2012. *A Burial of Sight* was first published by Wordhoard in 2012. *Blue Black* was first published by Mossley Hill in 2013. *Blood Child* was first published by Pavilion Poets, Liverpool University Press, in 2015. *Riverine* was first published by Gatehouse in 2015. *The Well at Winter Solstice* was first published by Salt in 2019. *Tam Lin of the Winter Park* was first published by Guillemot Press in 2022.

'The Hill' was first published in *Poetry Ireland Review*, 2023. 'In the Woods at Caerdeon' was first published in *Smoke*, 2023. 'Five Breaths' was first published in *Wild Court*, 2024. 'Quarried Stone' was first published in *Poetry Wales*, 2024. 'In Birchen Head' was first published in *Ambient Receiver*, 2024.

With thanks to the Eric Gregory Awards, The Society of Authors, The Forward Prizes, Irish Glen Dimplex New Writers Awards, Arts Council England, Arts and Humanities Research Council, University of Exeter, Liverpool Hope University, Northern Writers' Award for Poetry, The Windows Project and the literary communities of Merseyside, and to family and friends for all their support. Special thanks to Dave Ward.

Eleanor Rees was born in Birkenhead, Merseyside in 1978. Selections of her poems have been translated into Lithuanian, Slovak, French, German, Romanian and Spanish (Versopolis, 2016, 2019, 2024). Eleanor wrote her PhD at the University of Exeter, entitled *Making Connections: The Work of the Local Poet*, and is now senior lecturer in Creative Writing at Liverpool Hope University. She lives on the Wirral peninsula.

GUILLEMOT PRESS